THE
SUCCESSFUL
PITCH

CONVERSATIONS ABOUT GOING FROM
INVISIBLE TO **INVESTABLE**

JOHN LIVESAY

Foreword by **Judy Robinett**, author of *How To Be A Power Connector*

TRADECRAFT

Tradecraft Books, Los Angeles 90046
© 2016 by Tradecraft Books
All rights reserved. Published 2016
Printed in the United States of America
14 13 12 11 10 09   5 4 3 2 1
ISBN 978-0-9822853-5-0   0-9822853-5-3
Livesay, John.
The Successful Pitch: Conversations About Going From Invisible To Investable.

Book cover and interior design: Sergio Belletini
Author photo: Marcella Kerwin

In memory of my beloved King Charles Cavalier Spaniel, Buddy, who sat on my lap quietly and kept me company while I recorded these podcasts.

THE SUCCESSFUL PITCH

"When John Livesay appeared on my CBS News health segment, he shared with my viewers the connection that the more confident you are the healthier you become. His tips are unique and memorable. We all know you have to be confident when you pitch for anything. He has also helped me with my pitch for my own startup and gave me my own unique story that is compelling and concise. When it comes to
The Successful Pitch, *John is* **The Pitch Whisperer!***"*

Sudip Bose MD, FACEP, FAAEM

• Chief Medical Officer & Co-founder of *liveClinic, Inc.*
• Featured physician on hit worldwide reality TV show *"Untold Stories of the ER"*
• Iraq war veteran, recognized as a "CNN Hero" for receiving the Bronze Star and serving as the US physician who treated Saddam Hussein after his capture
• Recognized as one of the "Leading Physicians of the World" by the International Association of Healthcare Professionals

"John Livesay helped me pitch myself to the producers of 'Ellen' to be a guest. Their objections were that Ellen didn't have beauty segments or authors on her TV show. I was a beauty expert with a beauty book to promote. John helped me overcome those issues with creative storytelling that included the right pitch at the right time. That pitch worked and I got on 'Ellen.' From that first yes, I went on to become her beauty expert appearing numerous times over the last eight years. If you want to learn how to make a successful pitch, then read this book!"

Kym Douglas TV personality *Ellen/Home & Family*

CONTENTS

JUDY ROBINETT
FOREWORD

Having been a judge on many panels around the world, including one with Mark Cuban, where founders pitch to investors, I know that a solid pitch is rare. When I hear one, I know the company is fundable. Why? Besides showing me a good idea, the company has identified the exit and mitigated perceived risks, including a core team that can execute a sound go-to-market strategy. Paul Graham of Y-Combinator fame says there are two reasons startups fail: first is lack of a customer, second is lack of funding. Both of these risks can be addressed by a good team with a good strategy.

A good pitch is one that makes you want to know more. I like to say that the whole purpose of a pitch is to "get the second date," which usually involves investors saying, "Tell me more" or "We want you to come back and pitch in front of more of the investors in our group or company."

The problem is that only 1% of pitches ever get funded, usually because the founder is in the wrong room with the wrong story. I remember one occasion when a doctor pitched his medical device to our panel for over twenty minutes, and we still had no clue what he was talking about. When I asked the doctor some questions, he finally said, "This device helps doctors fix a hole in the heart." Bingo! At least now we were clear on what he was asking us to fund. No matter how complicated the idea or product is, you need to be able to explain it in a concise and compelling manner to the people you are asking to give you money.

The ability to help entrepreneurs create clear, compelling pitches is John Livesay's special genius. When John invited me to be on his podcast, *"The Successful Pitch,"* in April 2015, I could not have imagined we would become friends and business partners. But we connected immediately and realized we shared a passion for helping startup founders get funded. Soon after the podcast, I began referring people to John so he could coach them on their pitch. The feedback was fantastic and people's confidence soared. He is able to take a complex concept and boil it down to its essence, so investors not only understand it but are hungry to know more.

In September 2015, I invited John to join my team at Crack the Funding

Code, which is a virtual incubator for startups, where we help founders develop a funding strategy, craft a compelling story and gain warm introductions to the right investors. Angels, not venture capitalists, fund ninety percent of high potential startups. And now we see family offices doing direct deals, avoiding having their money tied up in funds or the stock market.

One of our clients, Cole Smith, came to us with no pitch deck and no connections. Working with him on his pitch, John helped Cole explain how his mobile platform could help saves lives in schools by instantly informing first responders and parents when there was an emergency, as well as giving them a color-coded floor plan of where the problem was occurring. In this case, saving time really could save lives, as well as giving parents and teachers the peace of mind of having a security and communications plan in place.

Since the leader of the team (the jockey) is a key element of the pitch, John had Cole explain how his military security background overseas made him the ideal person to execute this concept. We made sure his financial projections were based in logic and then had him practice his pitch with us.

When Cole was ready, I introduced him to an angel investor who invited him to pitch to the SLC Angel Group. He was given only ten minutes of pitch time and then ten minutes of Q & A. We prepared Cole to explain his concept in the allotted time and helped him craft answers to the questions he would most likely be asked.

Cole got the second date! He was asked to come back and pitch to a larger group of angel investors for ten minutes, with a thirty minute Q & A this time. Following this pitch, he received an offer and went into due diligence. The investors told him that his deck and presentation were in the top five percent of any they had ever seen.

Based on Cole's success in Salt Lake City, I was able to get him in to present to the New York Angels, a very large and prominent investor group. They were impressed that he already had an offer of funding, and they began to court him with their connections to the FBI that could help him scale up fast.

One of the questions the New York Angel investors asked Cole was who would be funding his next round. This is where most founders fail. However, I had introduced Cole to Claudia Iannazo, who sat on the board of Pereg Ventures, an early-stage venture capital firm. Claudia has connections to Jet Blue Airways, so I thought she would be interested in taking Cole's platform to airports once he needed Series A venture capital funding a year or so down the line. Both Angel groups were very happy that Cole already had a relationship with a venture capitalist, even though he would not need venture capital until he hit certain milestones that he hoped to do with their investment.

As this book is going to press, Cole has received his first Angel funding, and John and I are working with him during his due diligence process. We also connected him to the Los Angeles Unified School District and UCLA hospital for potential new clients. And we have been able to get Cole on three podcasts, which provides social proof for his pitch deck.

Cole is a great example of what the Crack the Funding Code team does for each of our clients. Twice a week, John and I are on the phone with our founders, helping them with strategy and having them practice their pitches. I have seen firsthand how John helps founders go from stumbling through their pitches to soaring through them, from confused investors to inspiring Angels who want to invest and join the team. John's secret sauce is having people tell stories that are memorable and that show the founders' qualities of tenacity and grit. Once you have a compelling story, you will usually get the second date.

Albert Einstein once said, "You have to learn the rules of the game. And then you have to play better than anyone else." That's true of anyone looking for funding — but it's also true of John Livesay. John's podcast has allowed him to grow his network of investors. He and I also co-host a private Facebook group for the guests so that investors from around the world who may not know each other can have a place to connect and potentially create deals together. Certainly, there's no one better than John when it comes to teaching you the rules of the game for a great pitch and how to pitch it better than anyone else.

Having a successful pitch opens many doors. My wish for you is that you learn the secrets and tips from the conversations in this book so that you too can get your startup funded — fast.

Judy Robinett, author of *How To Be A Power Connector*

INTRODUCTION
MY WORST MOMENT

Six months after I launched my business as *The Pitch Whisperer,* where I teach founders how to pitch for funding, I had the worst moment of my life as an entrepreneur. I had spent a great deal of money defining my avatar, finding the pain points around pitching, and realizing I was solving a big problem: only 1% of pitches to investors getting funded. In addition to that, I invested in creating a sales funnel with Facebook ads, a landing page and webinar which gave me leads who had no money and/or saw no value in hiring me. After 76 no's in a row, I thought I had wasted all my time and money. I was used to rejection from a twenty year career in sales, but I knew something was wrong. Either I had the wrong target market or the wrong offer. Was I crazy to think that founders who were pre-revenue would pay to get a great pitch to get funded, or was I missing something? I made the decision to not give up and dig further. Turns out founders know what they need and want help with a great pitch, but they also really want to get warm introductions to the right investors. After hearing that request dozens of times and always saying, "I don't do that or I don't know investors," I decided to launch my podcast *"The Successful Pitch"* and interview investors who would share their criteria with me on what makes a great pitch. I knew that I could then refer people that I've vetted to these investors.

I still had to conquer the fear of not getting any guests to come on without any episodes to listen to, or worrying about nobody downloading it if I spent more money to launch the podcast, but I took a leap of faith in myself and did it.

Like everyone who has ever thought of trying something new from launching a new business to learning a new skill, I, too, had to confront what I call the Three Faces of Fear. Clearly, fear can be a huge problem to overcome. The most important step in problem solving is clearly defining the problem in the first place. Many of the people you'll be reading about in this book talk about fear, but here's my take on it.

First: FEAR OF REJECTION—whether you are asking someone out on a date or asking an investor to fund your startup, people worry about being rejected. When I started The Successful Pitch, I was worried that people might reject my invitation to be on the show. The only way to conquer this fear is to refuse to take rejection personally. If someone says no to your offer, it just means it is not a fit now, not forever. The way to not take rejection personally is to not reject yourself. If someone says they don't like your idea for a new business, that does not mean you have to agree with their rejection. Famously, Howard Schultz was rejected many times before launching Starbucks—that is worth remembering.

Second: FEAR OF FAILURE—these are the internal thoughts you have when you launch a new business. When I was thinking about launching The Successful Pitch, I worried about the many forms of failure. All kinds of doubts and questions came up for me: What if nobody downloads any of the episodes? What if I can't find someone to help me edit the podcast? What if I spend all this time and money on a podcast and it flops?

The best way to deal with fear of failure is play out the worst case scenario in your head and say "So what?" Will I die of humiliation or will I regret not taking a chance?"

Third: FEAR OF THE UNKNOWN—if we only do the same things over and over, sticking only with what we know, we crush our soul's spirit to create and grow. The idea of a comfort zone is an illusion. If we are not constantly increasing the size of our comfort zone, it shrinks. There is no such thing as staying in the same spot, since change happens all around us. We have to choose to resist or to embrace the unknown.

When I started my podcast, the list of things I didn't know was a mile long: I didn't know how to properly interview people. I didn't know how to record a podcast or how to promote a podcast.

The good news is I found Harry Duran, an expert who trained me and was able to get my podcast listed on iTunes *"New & Noteworthy."* The podcast has allowed me to meet all kinds of wonderful and inspiring people who are changing the world with their innovations and courage as well as increasing my network. This book is my opportunity to share many of their stories with you.

My second guest on *"The Successful Pitch"* was Judy Robinett, who sits on the board of Illuminate Ventures. She started referring people to me to get my help with their pitch. After three months of the referrals getting great results, she invited me to join forces in Crack the Funding Code, where I help with the pitch, while she helps with the strategy and financials. She has referred many investors to me as guests on the podcast, which now complete our full offering of the right pitch to the right investors. Because of how important Judy has been to me in this adventure, I asked her to write the foreword for my book. So, let me say here, thanks for everything, Judy!

A big "a-ha" moment came when Judy told me, "I just read the greatest book. It's called *Disrupt You!,* and it was written by Jay Samit." I said, "Judy, I recently interviewed him on my podcast. Would you like to meet him?" This exchange encapsulates the synergy I'm trying to communicate in this book. Of course, Judy said yes, and that made me start thinking. What if we can network this way? What if my podcast can enable me to connect like-minded, successful people? Around this same time, Judy and I began to co-host a private Facebook group for the guests of my podcast. That way, investors and authors from around the world could get to know each other, and we could start our own ecosystem where investors can network and fund deals together. It turned out to be a huge success and has helped me get high quality guests on the podcast.

From Invisible to Investable

What I have learned from interviewing over eighty guests is that a successful pitch has certain key elements:

1. Grab their attention in the first ninety seconds. Just because you have ten minutes doesn't mean you have their attention unless you grab it at the beginning. The best way to do that is to offer a statistic that makes them intrigued to learn more.

2. Have passion when you present. You have to get yourself ready like an Olympic athlete and practice before you pitch. The goal is not to get rid of the butterflies in your stomach, but to get them to fly in formation.

3. Don't take rejection personally. I cannot overstate how important this is. The key to having a high level of resilience is to never reject yourself or your idea based on one person's feedback.

4. Be confident but not arrogant. Investors want to see founders who are coachable and who will take not just their money but their ideas. The

best way to increase your confidence is to "stack your moments of certainty." When you write down all the moments in your life when you were certain you nailed it and stack them before you pitch, your confidence will soar. It can be anything from interviewing for a job and knowing when you walked out you would get an offer, to winning an award to going on a first date and knowing you would get another one.

One of my clients, Martijn Atell, stacked his moments of certainty and it changed his life. He told me he grew up in the Netherlands but was born in South America. When he turned eighteen, his parents took him back there and dropped him off in the Amazon jungle for two weeks to survive because in his culture that is the right of passage into manhood. When I asked him what lessons he learned, he said he learned how to focus, pivot, and persevere. Then I helped him craft his story and told him to take those lessons from the Amazon jungle to the concrete jungle of being an entrepreneur. When he had that practiced, he won a pitch contest. Investors hear so many pitches, but that story is memorable, and they know if he can survive the Amazon jungle, he can survive anything. This story shows Martijn's tenacity and grit without him having to say he is someone with grit.

If you want to go from invisible to investable to potential investors, here is how to do it, rung by rung. Dating and pitching for funding have many things in common. The average marriage lasts about seven years, whereas an investor relationship can last ten years or more.

When you begin with just an idea, you are invisible. Investors don't know you exist. The same is true in some dating situations. You see someone at a party you are attracted to you, but they don't even know you exist. You are in essence invisible to them. Your chance: zero percent.

Next, you start to get a team together and work on your idea, but you have not tested to see if anyone wants the idea. You are slightly higher on the ladder at the more or less insignificant rung. From a dating perspective, I am not sure which is worse, invisible or insignificant. They may see you, but they have no real interest in you whatsoever. Your chance: twenty-five percent, at best.

But things are starting to get interesting. Now you have a minimal viable product with some interest from the marketplace. You and your team are getting traction and you start to become interesting to investors. They will say keep me updated, but are not interested enough to invest. In the dating world, maybe you say something amusing or clever and you get someone's interest. They still are not ready to go out with you. Your chance: fifty-fifty.

But now you have reached an intriguing rung: you have a great pitch, you have some interest from more than one investor, and you become intriguing. You are now at seventy-five percent. Investors will say that they're interested in starting some serious due diligence with you. In other words, you scored a date.

The top of the ladder is where you are irresistible. You get multiple offers; the investors start competing with each to get you to pick them. They talk about their connections and previous successes. The best way to get here is to leverage FOMO—fear of missing out—which is created so that investors see an urgency to invest with you now. The sense is "this train is leaving the station; if you want on, you better do it now."

I interviewed Charles Michael Yim, the only person in the history of "Shark Tank" to get all five sharks to invest. He created the Breathometer, which measures blood-alcohol level so you know if you should drive or not. He told me he presented everything through the problem/solution lens. The judges saw that he understood the problem well and that he had the unique solution. In the dating world, this is when you have more than one person courting you!

What I've put together for you here is a collection of the best conversations I've had with the world's experts, people who have heard thousands of pitches. As Plato says, "Storytellers rule the world." This book will teach you how to be a master story-teller. Then you can pull people in with your stories instead of having to push yourself on them by selling. Forget selling; tell stories.

Before we get to the conversations, let me sum up a few things for you about successful pitching. There are so many mistakes founders make when pitching that send up a red flag. Here are a few to avoid:

1. Never say, "We have no competition." If you don't have competition, you don't have a market. You need to have barriers to entry from your competition in place too.

2. Also, don't try this: "If we get just one percent of the entire population to buy our product, we will be rich." This is what is known as a top-down strategy. Investors want to see a bottom-up strategy which explains how you are going to drive sales with a targeted marketing plan.

3. Don't get caught without traction or proof of concept. If you're selling dog food, investors want to see the dogs eating the dog food. You need to have tested your concept to see if people will not only want it, but will pay for it.

4. Never admit, "We have no exit strategy. " Investors want a three hundred to five hundred percent return on their investment in three to five years. The fastest way to make that happen is grow fast and have a strategy on who could buy you.

5. Never admit, "We have no advisors." Investors invest in the jockey, not the horse. Having a strong advisory board and team are key factors in getting funded. Most founders think investors want to invest in the idea or product (the horse), but they don't know how to sell themselves (the jockey) as the right person to execute the idea.

6. Don't exhibit lack of preparation or lack of confidence. Sometimes founders think they can "wing" their pitch and not practice it. They come across nervous and unprepared. Never do that.

The Picasso of Pitches

Everyone knows that the best pitch paints a picture. So let's have you become the Picasso of Pitches.

Five years ago, I had the opportunity to meet Francoise Gilot in her charming New York apartment. She is the mother of Paloma Picasso and lived with Picasso during the 1940s; she's a painter in her own right, and her apartment was beautifully decorated with her work as well as Picasso's. It was like she lived in an art gallery. She speaks with a charming French accent and has a light that sparkles in her eyes, even though when I met her she was in her late eighties. She said to me, "During the 1940s there was a shortage of canvas because of the war." This meant that artists had no choice but to paint over their masterpieces. She said it very matter-of-factly with no remorse or sadness. She looked at one painting and said to me, "That is the fifth painting I painted on this canvas. I think the third one under it is my favorite." I asked, "What does it feel like to paint over your masterpieces?" She replied, "When you have to express yourself, you can't stop yourself. I still hold the memory of what I created in my mind and that is really where art lives after all."

To me it was sad that the world would never get to see her favorite painting that was long ago painted over and lost forever. However, the story has stayed with me all these years.

I get to share it with people who then are inspired to "paint over their masterpieces"—this is what startups mean when they speak of the "pivot."

Even when you have a shortage of materials in your startup, you still have the urge to create something that is your unique expression. Some creations become world famous and change the world, and some are secrets known only to the person who created it. Are you showing as much passion and drive to investors as an artist like Francoise Gilot did, so that your pitch makes an emotional connection like a piece of art? So, are you willing to paint over your Picasso? You have to, if you want to become the Picasso of pitches. If so, then this book will help you paint your best masterpieces to make your pitches a successful work of art.

The incredible people who have agreed to be on "The Successful Pitch" share a unique collection of experience, insight, and wisdom. My hope is that will you enjoy reading what they have to say as much as I did when I had the pleasure of asking them how they achieved their success and what the secrets are to having a successful pitch.

GUY SPIER
LUNCH WITH WARREN BUFFETT

Guy Spier is an ardent disciple of Warren Buffett. Guy has run the Aquamarine Fund for the last seventeen years. He launched the fund with fifteen million dollars in assets, very closely replicating the structure and approach of Buffett's original partnerships. Guy was educated at Oxford University, where he was a tutorial partner of former British Prime Minister David Cameron and was the top of his class in Economics. After his stint in management consulting, he attended Harvard Business School, and then worked as an investment banker before starting his own fund. He's a regular commentator in the media, and has appeared in CNN, in Bloomberg Television, as well as many other important places. He is also the author of an amazing book called *The Education of a Value Investor.*

John: Let's start early, before your career, even before Oxford. Did you have a personal passion for economics and investing as a child? What got you interested in all this?

Guy: That wasn't the case for me at all, John. The only time that I heard something investing-related was when we were living in Iran. Funnily enough, I remember the stock symbol. My dad was working for a German chemical company, and my father had opened up a brokerage account with Merrill Lynch in the United States, and he was following IBM. He would pick me up and I would sit next to him, and he'd make me look in the newspaper to find out what IBM share price had done on a day-to-day basis.

But, other than that, I had no contact with the stock market until, really, my final year at business school. Then, actually, the guy who was interested in it was a classmate of mine that I was doing a project with, whom I write about in my book. He's now really well-known. He's the CEO of Zinger. He wanted me to go in with him to buy Philippine Long Distance, a Filipino telephone company, and I said yes, so that was the first time that I started talking about the stock market with somebody at business school. It was really in my last year, and after I'd already seen Warren Buffett speak in my first year, so I suddenly said, "Oh, I want to go into finance." Now, I have to tell you, John, I was twenty-six at the time, so I wasn't that young. Warren Buffett was about a decade younger than me when he got going with investing the stocks. I have to say, at the time, and I wouldn't have admitted it to anyone, but it was all about greed. I fancied myself as a little Gordon Gekko, and I'm not proud of that.

John: Well, you transformed yourself, so that's fine, right?

Guy: It's easier to talk about it when you're something different. That's true.

John: One of the things that I really want to ask you about is this fascination of where did you find the money? Did you find it was a good investment? And tell us about how you were part of a charity fundraising charity event and bought an opportunity to have lunch with Warren Buffett, right?

Guy: My story, I think, is far less inspiring in that regard in comparison to this other guy that I write about a lot in the book, my friend, Mohnish Pabrai. In my case, I'd gone to this investment bank, D.H. Blair, and it really ruined my reputation, because it was an unsavory place that was ripping off orphans and widows. It would be the short way of talking about it. I really ought to have left within five minutes, but I actually stayed eighteen months. When I finally left, people did not want to offer me a job, and I went two or three rounds in a number of interviews, and then people just shut down, and I knew it was because they could see that I had those stains. I saw that in my book. I toyed with calling it a stain. A bloody stain like Lady Macbeth. It felt horrible to me. It felt like I couldn't wash it off, and nobody wanted to hire me.

In my case, my dad—and don't ask me why he did it—decided to gamble the substantial portion of his life savings on his son, and he came along and he said, "Look, I think you should try and start a business and I'm willing to be your key client to do it." I think that I'm quite an entrepreneurial type, but with my dad and the proportion of his net wealth that I knew he was investing with me, unless he had something stashed away somewhere else that he hadn't told me about, I knew that I couldn't mess this up, and I was once in awe of his willingness to trust me, and at the same time, I was scared stiff. And I still, to this day, don't fully understand why he did that.

But then I think, John, the thing is there are so many difficulties in life. What I realized now—I didn't want to accept it then—but if you should take the help from wherever it comes, and there's so many people who are using whatever advantage they have, and I realize now, in many ways, I had all sorts of disadvantages. I was an immigrant into the UK. I was kind of an immigrant into the United States. There are many people who had deep-rooted family and other kinds of connections that they were using. So if my dad was going to help me, that was perfectly legitimate and that was alright, and I think it's something that I didn't realize at the time, but to anyone starting a business, do not be afraid to accept help from those close at hand if that's the help that's available. Take what you have and use it. But, what I would say, John, is that I think the fact that that was my original source of money delayed me for about five or six years in terms of really learning how to sell myself. I didn't really understand how to do that. So, it came with that kind of disadvantage, if you like. It got me going, but then I didn't know how to scale from there.

John: Interesting. I love that insight: "Accept help from wherever you can get it, and don't be embarrassed about it." One of the things you describe in your book is how you spent a fortune, $650,000, to have one meal to meet Warren Buffett. How'd you find the money and what's that story?

Guy: Let me preface it by saying that it was before the financial bubble burst, and I had two or three very good years. So I wasn't spending money that I didn't have, and it's important that I was one-third of that sum; my friend Mohnish Pabrai came up with two-thirds of that, and I'd gotten to know him and he came up with this idea. Like you, I was like, "You want to do what? You want me to participate?"

And this is the thing, John, how can something that can sound so ridiculous, suddenly when you listen to the right person talking about it and their clearheaded thinking becomes actually something that's quite obvious, and quite straightforward. My reaction was the same as yours, and then Mohnish Pabrai, at this breakfast at the Mandarin Hotel overlooking Central Park, takes me through why it's a really smart thing to do. Before we can get into all the reasons why, I can tell you that in terms of return on that $650,000, if you like, the people that I've gotten to meet. It's not just you saw that photograph of my wife with Bill Gates, which is really wonderful. I can't say we had a long conversation with him, but even just that photograph with Bill Gates is very special. But below that, there are dozens of people I would never have met had I not gone to that lunch with Warren Buffett. It's not that Warren Buffett introduced me to them, it's that there are just a lot of people who wouldn't mind meeting the guy who paid $650,000 to have lunch with Warren Buffett.

What I understood beforehand is that it all comes down to the very special personality of Warren Buffett. So, it wasn't just a sort of, "Let me meet you for half an hour and then I'll run off." He hung out with us for about three and a half hours. He came determined in a degree. It was unnerving actually.

I mean, here's a guy who's one of the world's richest men. He doesn't have anything that we could give to him, and all he wants to do is serve us. All he wants to do is make us feel like we got so much value for it. That came afterwards. We showed up in Omaha one year early for the Berkshire meeting, and he invited us up into his office. He gave us a tour of his office. We hang out. Then he introduced us to Tracy Britt, who is now one of these "30 under 30" women. She's a rock star. She's very heavily involved in the next generation of Berkshire Hathaway managers, and he says, "Tracy, why don't you just come to lunch with us?" So, he's been delivering value, and he invites us to this brunch every year, where you get to hang out with people. I mean, one year, Charlie Rose was there. Bill Gates is there every year. He delivered enormous amounts of value, and it's changed my life, it's changed my network. But also just to witness that, what does it say to you and me, and a whole bunch of other people that if Warren Buffett, at his level of success, is humbly trying to deliver value to some guy who won a charity auction with him, can you imagine what he's like with his friends? It's not like I'm in his inner circle or anything, but I don't think he's any different, and so that really taught me that I had to have tremendous humility with all sorts of people, not just because it's a good way to be, but because it's incredibly rewarding, and it's a smart business. I mean, look at what I'm doing now. I'm taking time just to talk about Warren Buffett. It gets me so excited to think about it. The ultimate in being immense, being a good person, which will generate massive business rewards is to do stuff for people where there's no way they could ever thank you, you know? Because it's the kind of thing that they could not reciprocate.

Let me give you of an example of this in my work. I was giving a talk recently to the CFA society, and a guy there emailed me and asked if he could come by and get my book autographed. I said, "Sure," except I didn't realize that he didn't mean at the CFA talk, he meant that morning in my office. So, I get a knock on the door at the office, and I had some other things going on, but I realized that we had crossed wires and he actually wanted to come in the morning. Inspired by Warren Buffett, I said, "Alright, fine. I've met him. Now, I'm going to take half an hour. I made him a coffee. I did the Warren Buffett thing." This guy was a young student from Finland, and it was the same motivation. I wanted to make him feel like he got a surprising amount of value. I spent time with him at the library, I took photographs with him, we hammed it up a little bit, and I know that he's grateful to me, and he'll talk about that. I took photographs of it actually.

John: It sounds like, to me, that you've passed on what you learned from Warren Buffett to the next generation. The idea is to be humble with everyone you meet, regardless of who they are.

Guy: I would argue that the returns to the lunch with Warren Buffett, not just the network that I got to be exposed to, but then seeing him up close and seeing some things that were really surprising that I didn't really expect, was priceless. Like many people, I have a certain ego, and I feel like I'm quite a smart guy. There was some part of me that thought, "I may be as smart as Warren Buffett." Sitting with him, I just knew that I wasn't. I knew that he had a clocked speed that was higher than mine, and it was painful to experience that, and as this friend of mine, William Green, says, "weirdly liberating," because it freed me up. I was investing a lot of energy in trying to be something that I was not, and it is a waste of energy, and I knew I couldn't do it anymore. So I gave up that version of myself.

John: Well, just the freedom to not have to be the smartest person in the room all the time, I would think, would be very liberating.

Guy: Yes, it absolutely was, and not just liberating. I think that you use up brain cells that could be better used doing something else, thinking about whether it's your and your wife's anniversary, which it was yesterday. I didn't do very well with that.

John: Well, we won't let that ruin everything. You know, what you said to me, Guy, reminds me of this statement that I heard once, which is, "If you focus on being interested in the other person, as opposed to trying to be interesting to them, you'll have a much better conversation."

Guy: Yes, exactly. There's a story about the British Prime Minister Benjamin Disraeli: if you met him, you left thinking you were brilliant, but if you met another Prime Minister, Gladstone, you left feeling that he was brilliant. You want to be like Disraeli. It's not how you feel. It's how you make other people feel. Can you make other people feel good about themselves?

John: That's so useful for my target audience, who are probably in the position of going to pitch investors: if you make the investors feel good about themselves, investing in you as opposed to you trying so hard to impress them with how smart you are, you come across confident but not arrogant, and I think that's really what you're saying here. Let me ask you about the preparation you did. If you're going to spend that kind of money, over $650,000 to have lunch with somebody, I'm sure you were ready for that meeting. I'm talking to my clients all the time about the importance of preparing and practicing their pitch before they get in front of investors. I'm imagining that you put some thought and effort into the kinds of questions you were going to ask Warren during the lunch, right?

Guy: This is the funny thing, John. So, this is me to Mohnish Pabrai, who is way wiser than I am, and way smarter as well. I said, "Mohnish, shouldn't we prepare? Shouldn't we reread all of the publicly available information?" and he said, "You know, Guy, we've been studying." I mean, at that point, I'd been going to the Berkshire meeting for ten years. I was reading every single annual report. At the time, there was one biography that I'd read at least a couple of times and it was like, "Don't worry. The conversation will just flow." So, what Mohnish did, in investing in the lunch with Warren Buffet, was brilliant, and this is something that may be really valuable for everyone. What was billed as a power lunch became a sort of family occasion. So, Mohnish came with his wife and his two children, I came with my wife. It was very clear in a couple radio and TV interviews that we were just there to say thank you to somebody who's taught us a lot. These were all things to de-escalate the tension, de-escalate the sense of defensiveness that Warren might have.

Here's something that I just think doesn't work anymore in a hyper-connected world where everybody can reach for just about anything through

Google search, which is that the preparation of the pitch, in a certain way, it should be about saving the other guy time. It's not about trying to force them to listen to you, because they can find whatever they want. We can all find whatever we want. All of it's on sale on Amazon at a very low price. So, to save them time and to think about, "How do I reduce their sense of tension, their sense of defensiveness that will come up if there's something that's being asked for?" What's so wonderful about being around and studying somebody like Warren Buffett is that there are just so many valuable stories to land. For example, I'll tell you about Byron Trott, who's the only investment banker that Warren Buffett deals with. He has told it in a couple of interviews. He got this one-off meeting with Warren Buffett. Byron got about half an hour, and he'd flown out to Omaha. So he said, "Warren, give me a problem that you've got that nobody else has been able to solve. I can't guarantee that I will solve it for you, but I'd like to try."

So, here are all the things I love about that question. First of all, it says, "This meeting is about you. It's not about me. I want to hear what you have to say." So, it's offering something. It's offering your time to listen to what's on their mind. The other thing that it does is, instantly, without having to go through, it says, "I know that you already have a lot of great service providers. I know that you've got a lot of great stuff on your plate, and guess what? I don't want to compete with any of them because I'm sure that you're happy. I want your unsolved problems. If you've already got people solving your problems, I don't want to even start telling you that I can solve your problems better." I think that Warren Buffett is so brilliant. He heard that question, and he knew that he had a guy in his presence that he liked, because this guy was about Warren Buffett and his needs, not about what he was trying to pitch. Warren makes these decisions and, bang, Byron Trott was in his inner circle, and they've done I don't know how many deals. What Warren gave him, what he said to Byron Trott was, "Please, could you get me security issues that pay a negative interest rate." So we are paid to issue the security. It actually didn't work out financially. They had an embedded stock option in there that ended up costing Berkshire quite a bit of money. But, again, it got Warren's mind churning, and it makes me think of when I was a couple of years out of business school, I knew of a guy who got an internship with Warren Buffett. He wrote to Warren Buffett from Columbia Business School, and he asked for a job or for an internship, and then he included the check for his estimate of the amount of time that it would take Warren Buffett to read the letter. I don't think that Warren ever cashed the check, but what Warren loved was that this guy was thinking in the right way. He was thinking about that Warren's time was valuable and he didn't want to waste Warren's time, and he thought, "A guy who thinks like that is thinking in the right direction."

John: Well, it's a classic case of empathy, isn't it? You put yourself in Warren Buffett's shoes and you realize how valuable his time is, and you did a gesture that acknowledged that. The thing I love about the story you just told us of how he picked that investment banker, "Give me a problem that you haven't been able to solve." That is what everybody wants to hear in a pitch, "Tell me a problem that you're solving that no one else has solved yet, or that you're solving it in a way that is unique." It's disruptive, it's going to change the world, make the world a better place. So, on a one-to-one basis, if you can help somebody solve a problem and, of course, on a global basis, if you're looking for investment. That's such a great story and so helpful. I really want to dig in a little bit about what you wrote earlier in your book about "the more you understand yourself, the better of an investor you become." Can you elaborate on that?

Guy: Even before we get to investing, let's talk about teams. I'm sure that you've done it, many of us have done it. I've been in small teams. It's usually people who work for me, and there's a commitment that they've made and then they failed to meet it, and I realized that it's not for lack of desire. It's because they didn't understand who they really were and they didn't understand, and it's not that their communication with me was bad, that they were being dishonest or not trustful. It's that they didn't understand their deepest desires or they didn't understand their own capacities. I think that when you have somebody who shows up at work, it's so much nicer to hear somebody say, "You've asked me to set up this computer. I'm not very good at it. I'm not sure I'll succeed, but if you really want me to try, I will, but it's actually not my strong suit." This attitude really breeds trust and I think, in a certain way, if we come to investing, it's the same thing.

If I identify with my rational brain, I'm going to trip up. So I feel like I have these teammates inside me that I have to bring along. So, there's the rational brain, but then there's this emotional thing going on, which is raging around all over the place, and that, unfortunately, it's like a member of the team that you really wish you could lose but can't sometimes. So, I can't ignore that person. It's like you try and ignore that teammate and you try and put them in the corner and shut them up, but then they go and really wreak havoc.

John: Then they get mad.

Guy: Yes, so you have to find a way to involve them in a certain way, and I think that just being honest with myself, one of the examples I write about is that, unlike Mohnish Pabrai, I have this inordinate fear of loss. I don't want to have to start from scratch, and I'm more fearful, I think, than many people of losing money. So, I don't think that it would have made sense to ignore that. I think I had to be honest with myself and with my investors and say, "You know, if I was utterly rational, this is a great investment. But you know what? It scares the hell out of me, and I can't sleep with that." So, I'm not going to worry about it, even if it means that my returns will be lower.

John: Right. Know yourself and then know your own risk tolerance. If you're an entrepreneur, you have to be comfortable with your own risk. You might be risking not having a steady paycheck for a while, and what if your company doesn't do well or whatever it is, you have to know yourself and your own comfort zone, and I love what you say about thinking of all the different parts of our brain, left brain, right brain as members of a team as opposed to fighting ourselves. We're all on the same team here, so let's figure out how we can best work together instead of shutting everybody up.

Guy: It's like I think that we've all been through these times where we fight with the forces that are arrayed around us in the universal. Like Jacob struggling with the angel, it just doesn't work very well. It works much better when we align ourselves with those forces. Then, in a strange way, actually, when you talk about—if you don't embrace the risk or you don't embrace the fear saying, "You'll do this, this is great. I'm fearful or you'll do this. This is great." It's like because I see the risks so clearly or because I feel the fear so much, this is motivating me to take all these actions. So, if I'm not honest with myself about my fear of loss, or if an entrepreneur is not honest with himself about the very real possibility of failure, we're not going to be motivated to do everything we possibly can to make it succeed. The strange thing for me is that the times when I've been in those kinds of circumstances, on the one hand, I feel utterly alive. You know, actually, writing the book was a bit like that. And then, on the other hand, it's like once I'm through it, I'm like, "I don't want to go through that again."

John: I understand. In fact, I wrote a whole blog about starting a podcast and the three faces of fear that I had to overcome. The fear of rejection, the fear of failure, and then the fear of the unknown. For me, identifying those fears into three faces helped me deal with them. So, it wasn't just any kind of fear. I would say, "Which fear is this?"

Guy: But there's something else that I think is so incredibly critical. I learned this from a friend of mine who's a psychologist: emotions are a call to action, and if we don't feel those emotions, we're not going to take the action that we need to take. So, I would argue, I felt it as you were saying it that the fears that you were dealing with, it wasn't that you were just dealing with them, they were motivating you to do stuff. If you didn't feel that, you wouldn't have done as good a job in setting up your podcast.

John: Emotions are a call to action. I love that.

Guy: They're two sides of the same coin, you know. I was just listening to the Brené Brown TED talk with a couple friends the other day. It was about how the vulnerability is what gets the healing, is what gets the result, and we just can't have the one without the other.

John: It's so true. Earlier you and I were speaking about your sense of liking to help people, especially founders, possibly even get funded so that when they sell their company, they'll remember you. Talk to me about how that all works in your world.

Guy: I'll tell you because it's just amazing the way it started. It started out of a really venal place, which wasn't generous at all. I'd read Robert Cialdini's book, Influence: The Psychology of Persuasion, and it's got this great story about these Hare Krishna money raisers who would hand out plastic flowers in airports. The human reciprocation tendency is so strong that even if you hand out plastic flowers, then you still will feel obligated to give something is very effective. So, I'm thinking, "Damn, I can use this." So, I'm in New York and I'm giving the doorman a piece of candy; I'd carry sweets or chocolates around with me. I'd be giving stuff to people all the time, but I wasn't coming out of a place of love for humanity or of generosity. I was coming out of a place of pure manipulation. I was like, "Let's see how I can manipulate people to do stuff for me," and all sorts of things happened as a result of that. But, really, this is part of why I wanted to write the book: I suddenly found that I actually enjoyed it, not because I could manipulate them into doing something, but because I realized that people genuinely responded, even to my fake giving. I know, over time, I think my fake giving turned into something which was much more genuine.

Then, over time, what happened was that I started wanting to do it on a larger scale. I have a friend who starts medical technology companies in Minnesota, and I suddenly realized that I was coming across people that he would be interested to meet, and it sort of tapped into the same idea of finding a way to be generous because good things come back to me if I'm generous.

Actually, I'll give you a story. I'm a member of this group called the Entrepreneurs' Organization which, is fantastic. So, I helped start the Israel chapter. Again, this was my idea of wanting to help people but, with the idea that, at some point, these guys — some of them might build big businesses and have money to invest and then they might send some of that to me. One of the members is a woman who's looking for funding. Her name is Mikhail Lodski. She was looking for funding. I hadn't even met her. So here's what I did: I wrote up something, which said, "Dear, First Name, I'm a member of an organization called EO, and EO's has a member called Mikhail Lodski, and she's got what looks like a great business plan and I would be really grateful if you take a look at it." Then I wrote, "Look, I don't understand a lot about it, but if you were to at least take a look and see if you can help, it would mean a lot to me, and I would be grateful to you for that." Then I went into my LinkedIn profile and I did a search for 100 people who, in some way, were involved in the world that she was looking for funding in. They were either venture capitalists, or they were angels, or they were in that business, and I just cut and pasted that message like I don't know how many times, and you know what was interesting? It was unlike asking for it yourself; the fact that I was asking for it and they knew me, there was some connection, I'd met them at a conference or something. Even if they had no interest, they could see that I was doing this out of the desire to help somebody, so they accepted it in a way that if she'd gotten in touch with them directly, they wouldn't have, and then one of them actually took a close look, it was in their space, they liked it. They ended up funding her business.

John: What a great story. You can never underestimate the importance of a warm introduction. It's everything. It's been so wonderful hearing your stories and your personal transformations. Is there any last piece of advice you have for someone who's in the world of starting a business, looking for funding, or about life or business, in general, that you want to share as a closing thought?

Guy: What I would say, and the thing that I feel I've learned that is so important is always leave a little on the table, always generate more value than you take, always leave people wanting more. Then, just keep doing that for a decade. I told that guy who came and did an internship with me, I said, "If you help ten people, you've got a few friends. If you help a hundred people, you probably find a job. If you help a thousand people, you can probably start a business. If you help ten thousand people, you'll have quite a successful business, and if you start being in the range of helping a hundred thousand people, then you've got a substantial business. When it gets to a million, you're like Warren Buffett, and when it gets to ten million, you're like Mahatma Gandhi." But that's approximately the order of scale, and it's just about having how many people out there just feel grateful that you're on the planet.

John: What a great philosophy.

Guy: When you do that, good things will come to you. They may not be what you wanted. God might have other plans in store for you, but good things will happen.

John: It's just having that as the intention: "Generate more value than you take."

Guy: I want to reach out and give you a hug, John. This has been wonderful.

ANDREW GOLDNER
HOW TO CONNECT WITH A VENTURE CAPITAL INVESTOR

Andrew Goldner is the co-founder of GrowthX, a venture capital fund. He has a fascinating background from working at Thomson Reuter in Asia, to being a lawyer, to now being a Venture Capitalist. He has a whole explanation of what it takes to be successful, to get funded as a founder and the qualities they're looking for in a person, which include humility and the ability to focus. He was part of a team that won the Journalist of the Year award for Thomson Reuter in 2009. He's a mentor at Golden Gate Ventures and at Startup Mexico, helping innovators there.

John: I always like to have people tell us how they got to where they are, and certainly, we don't get many journalists becoming venture capitalists. So that's an interesting story. I'm guessing you had a passion for journalism and somehow it transitioned into shifting from telling stories to making them.

Andrew: It's actually a little bit different than that. I would love to claim myself among the profession of journalism. I'm not actually a journalist. At Reuters, I was the publisher, and so to a certain extent, I was a suit in the corner. But I had the distinct honor of working alongside some of the best journalists in the world at Reuters after Thomson and Reuters came together. I do think that I appreciate journalism and understand the rigors of journalism and I think I was fortunate, from that perspective, to connect with journalists. But, I, myself, am not a practicing journalist.

John: And yet you got honored with Journalist of the Year in 2009. How did that come about?

Andrew: That was very special. I mean, every year, Thomson Reuters and Reuters, historically, have gathered some of the best journalists from across the field. David Schlesinger, the editor-in-chief at the time, instituted something very new that year, which was pushing innovation in the newsroom. We were working on it together, and I was fortune enough to be working alongside of some of the top journalists in the Asia-Pacific region when we innovated around the idea of taking the Reuters messaging platform and bringing journalists into a chat room so that clients could interact directly with journalists as they were at the edge of news and provide an edge to those clients such as FX traders. It's something that we started regionally and ended up going global and it still operates today. So, at the time, pushing innovation and wanting to recognize it, David created that new award, and the team that I was fortunate enough to work with were awarded the Journalist of the Year.

John: Well, to me, it seems like the bridge between that award and what you're doing now is that it all stems from a passion for innovation.

Andrew: That's absolutely right, John, and I appreciate that perspective. I think if you look at my nonlinear path, I think there are a couple of themes that are consistent and, certainly, entrepreneurs and innovation is one of them. I try to do that inside of a law firm. I did that inside of Corporate America. I did that on my own. I've done that at early stage companies and now, of course, doing that at GrowthX. It was an extraordinary time to be at Thomson Reuters and to be associated with Reuters News. There was a tremendous amount of innovation that's gone on that continues to go on and, of course, the changes that are taking place in the media space are dramatic, and so innovation has certainly played a role.

John: Tell me about what you do at GrowthX and what makes it so unique. In part, the way you do seed funding has its whole premise that you and I talked about earlier, an idea I love, which is that you don't have to move to get funded.

Andrew: There are a couple of different components to the story of what we're trying to do at GrowthX. We want to try to keep it simple, but the reality is we are trying to innovate and do things differently, and so it's less of an obvious story. If you look at the history of GrowthX, we were born as a consulting firm that provided market development services to seed-stage startups. The idea is that seed-stage capital is plentiful nowadays, but, because the cost and complexity of launching a company and a product are so much less than they used to be, the reality is that you differentiate yourself at the early stages of a company. Nowadays, it's less about the product and more about how do you take that product, apply it to a market, go to market, find product market fit, earn predictable revenue, and scale. The reality is that, though seed stage capital is plentiful, the expertise in Silicon Valley and startup cities around the world in going to market, finding product market fit, earning predictable revenue is actually in quite short supply. So we started out as a consulting firm, earning both cash and equity. Through that work, we were able to prove that our market development expertise is actually a more valuable form of currency than investment capital because, as we were building that consulting firm working alongside venture capitalists, they were deploying money and getting a certain amount of equity in return, we were deploying our human capital and not only get compensated with cash, but we were earning significantly more equity than the angel and seed-stage investors were getting at that same time. That was really the genesis. GrowthX quickly grew from that into a venture capital model because we thought that there was a way to capture more value for everybody involved and align more long-term with everybody involved, and that includes the founders and the portfolio companies, the limited partners, the general partners, the co-investors. Everybody in our community, we think, is better aligned as a venture firm that invests dollars in human capital as opposed to just consulting services.

John: Tell me about some of the vision you have. I know you're starting to do some work in markets like Nashville and Dallas. Letting people live where they live and still get access to seed capital, what's the big vision for GrowthX?

Andrew: I appreciate you asking because it's obviously a lot more interesting than it is with the structure of the fund. The reason I bring it up is because they're related. The reality is we started out with the premise that you've been referring to, which is that you ought not to have to leave your home to build your company. The founders of GrowthX find it surprising that founders from around this country, and around the world, move themselves to one of the most expensive ZIP codes in order to position themselves better to raise money when, in reality, they're causing themselves to need to raise more money and for those people that have spent time in Silicon Valley.
It's a wonderful place, but it also is high-paced and can be a bit of a rat race, and so getting lost in Silicon Valley is an easy thing to happen to young founders. Our premise, then, is unless your customers are in Silicon Valley, why move here? There's more opportunity to work with developers in your hometown and leverage developers elsewhere. Keep the cost base low, stay focused, and let's see if we can bring venture capital to you.

When we broke it down and said, "Well, how do we solve that? How do we do that at scale?" Because of the economics of venture capital, it's what led us towards the model that I just discussed which is being local in these communities. Being insiders as opposed to outsiders, just visiting with a GrowthX team there that not only deploys capital and is an active member of the entrepreneurial community, but also can build a team of market development experts who can help these seed stage companies with the traction requirements that they're going to need to satisfy to then raise series A venture capital is how we're going about doing it. Our first office was opened up in Nashville. My partner, Brad Holliday is a twenty-year veteran of the space in around the southeast and so we were lucky enough to connect with Brad and have him as a partner in the fund, open our first office outside of Silicon Valley in Nashville, Tennessee, and we're very active around that state. Tennessee has done probably the best job of every state that we've been exposed to in terms of the intentional approach to using entrepreneurism to fuel economic growth. Launch Tennessee runs a network of accelerators around that state, and they're just doing a terrific job and, by the way, playing to their strengths, which is part of the theme as well. You have companies that are assuming they need to come to Silicon Valley to raise money or to accelerate their growth. But the reality is, again, unless there's a history of "been there done that" or the customer base here in Silicon Valley, why not go somewhere like Memphis if you're going to do logistics at the seat of FedEx. Or if you're going to do health tech or music, why not do it in Nashville. Or if you're going to do CPG, why not do it at The Brandery in Cincinnati, or if you're in retail, why not do it at REVTECH in Dallas with Nordstrom and Neiman Marcus. I think we're looking for opportunities to enable communities that are playing to their strength and enabling their startup communities. We want to play a very important role, not just as outsiders, but to be there and physically present.

John: Can you speak a bit about your other big disruptive shift in that everyone talks about the importance of the team and building a network of trust? But what I love that you said to me earlier was that your GrowthX is going to be featuring the founder's faces, as opposed to the logos of the companies that you're funding.

Andrew: What we've got up is just kind of a placeholder and we're being very serious about this website because it is going to be our face to the world, and we want it to embody all of these concepts that we're building the culture of GrowthX with. I think, typically, when you go to a fund website, you'll see the portfolio with logos. Our view is that it should be community and human-centric, and so our landing page is going to be filled with the faces of our founders. You'll be able to dig in and to read about and learn their stories and certainly hear about what they're working on now. But, ultimately, we're building a community of people. We refer to it as a trust network.

John: It's so great because when you have a trust network, then that's ultimately what the investors are investing in is you, and they have to trust and like you before they're going to invest in you. Most people lead with the product when they're pitching as opposed to leading with who they are.

Andrew: That's right. One of my co-founders at GrowthX is Will Bunker. Will is the founder of what became Match.com and, after exiting that, has become a very active angel and venture investor. He was doing a significant number of relatively small investments, and he came up with the idea of the trust network. Because the reality is when you're doing over a hundred different investments, which he has in his portfolio, at the pace he's making those investments, the only real way to do that is to build a network of trust and to do that by focusing on relationships and not transactions, so that as you're looking to do deals or as deals are brought to you, you trust the person who brought you that deal. You layer on a little bit of your due diligence, but you can make the quicker decision, and when you're looking at a deal and you want to act fast, you can look into your trust network and say, "Who is a subject matter expert that we can enable to help us think through this? Who are the co-investors that would be strategic or otherwise helpful to this company and how can we enable them to come in?"

Again, because we optimize for relationships and not transactions, we're not looking to take a piece of every relationship that we form. When we connect an LP in our fund to another fund, we don't look to benefit in any way other than helping to grow relationships. When our LPs invest directly in the startups in our portfolio, we don't force them to form a sidecar so that we can take a couple of different points of carry in addition to that which we have in our portfolio. When we introduce startups to other investors, we don't sharp elbow ourselves into a larger position. I know, by the way, if, ultimately, there's an investor who makes more sense than us then we're in for the long term. We're playing this long game and so if that particular opportunity doesn't pan out for us, that's fine because there's plenty of other opportunities, and if it works out for someone else in our community, we're just as happy.

John: That speaks to your character and, as you said, the long term vision and not forcing something that's not a fit and trusting that the right thing will be a fit. One of the things you wrote that I just love the analogy in An Astronaut's Guide to Life on Earth and, specifically, this whole concept of humility as it relates to a minus one, a zero, and a plus one. Can you talk more about that?

Andrew: That's something that came right out of the book that Commander Hadfield wrote, which was my inspiration for that piece. You know, again, when you enter into an organization, if you're striving too hard and too quickly to show off just how much value you can add or how smart you are, you end up distracting and detracting more than actually adding value, and a startup is an extraordinarily sensitive entity. It's one thing to step into an organization of fifty-five thousand employees; it's another thing to step into one with only five that's only been around for only a few months. One of the things that we talk about, and certainly something that we look for in the founders that we're investing in, is the idea that when you enter into something new, as odd as it may sound, you should really try to be that zero, to just try to sit and listen and learn. Don't be too quick to act. Don't be too quick to think that you have to show off your value or your intelligence. The most important thing is that you have a neutral impact until you're able to then add value and then reach for the opportunity to become a plus one. But, you know, as Commander Hadfield wrote, proclaiming your plus oneness at the outset virtually guarantees you're going to be perceived as a minus one regardless of the scales that you actually apply, regardless of how you actually perform. It is certainly a lesson that I've learned. I'm proud to apply it, and it's certainly something that we look for when we're speaking with founders.

John: Well, it's almost like if you say you're cool, you're not cool.

Andrew: Yes, I think, to a certain extent, that's true. I think humility is something that's very important. We're often asked at GrowthX, as a fund, of course, "What do you guys look for? What do you invest in?" and I think the answer they're searching for is, "Industries, sectors, stage, business model." Our answer is a little different. Our answer is it's very human-focused; our number one response is we're looking for founders who lack hubris. I'm biased. I grew up in Cleveland, Ohio, so I have a bias to Midwest and the life lessons that you learn at an early age growing up in the Midwest. I think humility is an important thing for people to have.

John: Well, I'm just supporting your bias because I'm from the suburbs of Chicago, and I also gravitate towards people from the Midwest. I think just growing up in an environment where there's so much snow and you just help your neighbors dig out of the snow. Speaking of that mindset, in addition to humility, you talk about attitude and focus in this great article. Can you speak a little bit about what kind of attitude does it take to keep bouncing back when things don't go right?

Andrew: Attitude really fortifies. I think it was Elon Musk who famously said that the startup adventure is like chewing broken glass while edging yourself toward the abyss. It's an extraordinarily uncomfortable thing. It's living minute to minute, hour by hour, day by day outside of your comfort zone. It's what makes it an extraordinarily difficult journey and when you're going through that and you're feeling not just the inter-month highs and lows. This isn't just the intra-week high and lows. This is the intra-day high or lows. From one hour to the next, you could go from cloud nine to the deepest of doldrums and you may simply have been set off by an email from a venture capitalist. What fortifies, what gets you through it is the attitude. There's going to be a lot of challenges and a lot of miracles between startup and success. The one trait, at least, that I've observed when I have met with entrepreneurs across continents, the thing that is the most common among them isn't the full stacked development skills. It's not their high IQ. It's just that orientation to stay calm and carry on.

John: Yes, I call it getting off the self-esteem roller coaster where you're going up and down.

Andrew: Very well put. When everything is flying high, when everything is going well, it's easy, right? But when you're facing the end of your runway, when you're not sure how you're going to pay your employees, when a deal that you were certain you were going to land and you were counting on ends up flipping the wrong direction, that's when true character shines.

John: Right, and in your final aspect, it's so important, especially running a company, to stay focused and not get distracted. You have some great insights on that.

Andrew: Well, it's a very difficult thing to do. I mean, honestly, there I'd refer to Greg McKeown and his book, Essentialism. It's a must-read for anybody who's an entrepreneur who asks me to suggest a book but for anybody that I speak to who's asking for advice on a book to read or who is struggling through what so many of us struggle through nowadays in the age of information and constant attention and awareness and access; that is, the ability to focus and prioritize. I think there are a lot of extremely powerful messages that Greg portrays through Essentialism. For me, one of the single strongest ones is the idea of being intentional in what your priorities are; otherwise, you'll find yourself spending most of your time working through other people's priority list.

John: Yes, that's so great because you're constantly reacting and you're not focusing on what you need to get done, so then you don't make any progress, right?

Andrew: Right. I like to share with people in the context of this type of conversation. I would no more ask you to subjugate your priorities to mine than I would accept you asking me to subjugate mine to yours, and though very few people, hopefully that you run into, are open and obvious about wanting you to subjugate yourself and your priorities to them and their priorities, the reality is that the subtleness of their behaviors or the subtleness of their reactions to your relationship, that's the message that comes through loud and clear. When they're impatient about an email response, when they're needing something fast, or when they want you to reply and they push you, the reality is that you have a set of priorities and you need to communicate those clearly to the people in your community and do so with respect and if those people don't show you the respect back and appreciate that you need to focus on your priorities and that you're looking forward to engaging when you have that opportunity, well, that's an invitation for someone to nurture themselves out of your community.

John: Yes, or out of your company because sometimes you can hire people who are so needy and impatient that they don't understand that you have other people to answer and other things to get done besides what they need done.

Andrew: That's absolutely right. I have this conversation often in the context of fundraising because not only do I spend all day every day with the fund and meeting with founders, but I also give a fundraising workshop. I do it as frequently as I'm invited, always helping founders understand how to avoid the number one mistake that I believe a founder makes when raising investment capital: the mistake of acting as if being busy is the same as making progress. In Silicon Valley now, for a variety of reasons, it's not difficult to get a meeting with an investor, but the reality is, is that investor aligned and is it an ideal investor for the story you're telling, the company you're trying to build, the stage you're at now? So I find, often times, a hand will go up in the audience at the workshop and, "Well, Andrew, I appreciate what you're saying but I've been working with one VC. I really want them on board. I'm really trying to help them understand the following things. They don't seem to understand it so I need to tell my story differently so I can help them understand these things, or the questions that they're asking don't seem to be relevant but I need to make sure they understand them because I have to get them on board," and my response is, "Listen, if you've taken the time and you've been thoughtful and intentional about defining, through logic, what the profile is of the investor that's going to be most likely to be interested in what you're doing now and it's consistent with the story you're telling and the company you're building, you know right away that this person you're speaking with, it's just not a relevant person for you to be raising money for right now." I say, be respectful, be polite, suggest that maybe this isn't the right opportunity, but you'd like the opportunity to engage later, and speak with the people that appreciate what you're doing and that get what you're doing and want to dig in from the right perspective as opposed to somebody you think is distracting.

In a roundabout way, I'm asking your question right back. I think this is how you focus. I mean, focus doesn't happen without being thoughtful and intentional about it and whether it's what I'm going to accomplish today in spending the first fifteen minutes of my day being thoughtful about what my priorities are and then being polite and transparent with everybody else to let them know what I need to focus on today and hope that they'll appreciate that and stay in the community or whether it's what I'm going to accomplish. I think the same applies in that the way that you stay focused is by being intentional about what your priorities are and whether it's a Post-it note on your monitor, a reminder app on your iPhone, whatever the case is, whatever it is that you need to do, keep it front and center.

John: I want to highlight two things you mentioned: Being busy is not equal to progress, and focus on the quality, not the quantity of, meetings you have with investors.

Andrew: I mean, I'm amazed at how often I am meeting with a startup and when I ask them what their fundraising strategy is, it is essentially to reach out to Google or Quora, find out what the top investors are in their geography or at their stage, to alphabetize those, to drop them into an Excel Spreadsheet or Google Sheet, to share that Google Sheet with their friends and invite everybody to please annotate it with who they have relationships with, the strength of those relationships, and their willingness to make an introduction. But at no point have they even stopped to consider whether that fund or that person is the right person for the story they're telling and the product they're building. Is this the right person? Is there a reason that they will be attracted to what you're doing, not just generally deploying capital?

So, for me, when I give my fundraising workshop or I'm speaking with entrepreneurs, I quote Albert Einstein and it's one of the few opportunities I have to quote Einstein, when he says if he had an hour to solve the world's problems, he would take fifty-five minutes to find the problem and only five minutes to solve it. I think that's one of the most important quotes because it reeks of intentionalism and that's a word that I probably overuse, but it seems so useful, especially in the context of moving at the speed of a startup. It's very easy to jump into action, but the reality is, by first spending a significant part of the time being intentional and defining what it is you're trying to accomplish before you jump into action, it can actually be more productive.

John: Well, you get a lot more rapport with someone if you show them the respect of doing a little bit of homework on who they are and what's important to them.

Andrew: I think that's right.

John: I do want to ask you about the Cargo Chief story about how hard it is to change people's behavior when you're putting a new product out.

Andrew: Cargo Chief is just a fantastic company. It's out of the Bay Area. The CEO and co-founder Russ Jones is an outstanding man with a proven track record. Essentially, Cargo Chief is the Saber of long haul trucking. Imagine if there were ten thousand different airlines and if you wanted to go from New York to Chicago, you had to pick up the phone and call each of them and ask them if they were going to Chicago and whether they had a seat on their plane and then keep calling until you found one that was going where you wanted when you wanted and, in many ways, that's how long haul trucking works currently. Cargo Chief is doing something extraordinary to innovate around that, so that they can know the lane and capacity of every truck on the road in America.

We started working with Cargo Chief and helping them to find their product market fit pretty early on. I think one of the things we identified from the outset was that when you're building a two-sided marketplace, when you are introducing an innovative product, you need to be careful not to drink too much of your own Kool-Aid, regarding just how innovative the product is. It might ultimately lead to efficiencies in cost savings or higher profits, but human behavior tends to trump everything else, and changing human behaviors is extremely difficult. One of the things that we have found with innovative products, especially in the marketplace, is that it's difficult to build up liquidity in that marketplace when you're forced to change your behavior from launch without having any true value to offer to or to be perceived by the customer. So the advice that we offer and, certainly, the work that we do at GrowthX when we're working alongside of select portfolio companies and helping them get product market fit, is to figure out how to engage current behaviors and provide a significant amount of value by engaging those current behaviors and then, over time, as you introduce more value and deliver more value, then you can begin to change behaviors.

John: I love the attitude, I love the intention, I love the focus, and, most of all, I love the message of humility because that requires a lot of emotional intelligence, which is what a true leader like you has.

Andrew: Well, thank you, John. I really appreciate it. I've really enjoyed this conversation.

TIM SANDERS
DEAL STORMING

Tim Sanders is a renowned entrepreneur, author, and speaker. Tim's book *Love is the Killer App* changed my life when I read it over a decade ago. I was so knocked out by the book that I reached out to Tim via email. We became friends, and I was honored and thrilled beyond belief that he was willing to write a foreword for my book way back then. He continues to inspire, not just me, but thousands and thousands of people around the world. He spent most of his career on the cutting edge of innovation and change. He was on the ground floor of the quality movement, the launch of the mobile phone industry, and today he's now all about disruptive change. He was an early stage member of Mark Cuban and Todd Wagner's Broadcast.com, which had the largest opening IPO in history. After Yahoo! acquired the company, Tim had a great title, the Chief Solutions Officer, and he was tapped to lead their value lab, which enabled sales teams to close hundreds of millions of dollars. By 2001, he was up and running as a leadership coach. Then, in 2005, he founded Deeper Media.

John: Nobody tells a story better than you, Tim Sanders. I've heard you speak live multiple times and you just grab the audience with these amazing stories that are not just funny and interesting, but have these great takeaways. Can you tell us how you became such a good storyteller?

Tim: I have been fortunate to live through a lot of really interesting stories. Over the course of time, I've always tried to learn something from every interesting encounter because a lot of times, stories are just that. They are problems, movement, encounters, and solutions. I began to really work earnestly on story development as I started to give more speeches on the lecture circuit because I needed to move audiences to action. I learned that as we tell stories, people are with you during your talk. If the story reinforces something, then they're willing to make a change.

I read a book around 2002 titled *Working the Room* by Nick Morgan. It's been re-titled since then by Harvard Business Press as *Give Your Speech, Change The World*. Nick blogs at PublicWords.com. I hired him to be my coach because he specializes in learning how to write a speech that is structured around one of the five archetypal stories, then learning how to use anecdotes, what most of us call stories, and how to use anecdotes to change the viewer or the attendee's perspective. He taught me that there are only five stories in the world. There's the love story. There's the revenge story. There's the hero's journey. There is the fish out of water, also known as the stranger in a strange land. Then, lastly, there is coming of age. That's it, and these five stories are deeply coded into our collective psyche, through mythology and storytelling, right? We know these stories inside and out.

As a communicator, if you think of your speech, or if you're telling an anecdote, if you think of your story as following one of those five lines, then it has a very predictable plot. It has a beginning, it has dynamics. It has a result, and the result has a moral to it, and the moral becomes actionable to the people who hear it. That's what I've worked on for a really long time. In my business, I write books, I give speeches, to help people change their perspective or validate their perspective. These stories move people.

I'll say this finally: perspective is just our story or stories about how the world really works. Whether that perspective is a religious belief, or a political ideology, or a business best practice, or an entrepreneurial habit, these are all based on the stories that are in our mind about how the world really works, right? What's successful? What does karma mean? All these things, which explains why stories are so powerful: they feed one's overall perspective.

John: That's great. It either helps you reinforce your perspective, or give you a new one. That's literally what you're trying to do when you're pitching an investor is to get them to think about something, your idea, or app, or product, in a way that they haven't thought about that would motivate them to want to write a check to you versus all the other pitches they're hearing in a day. You have a new book coming out called *Dealstorming*. I just think the title and where it came from is so fascinating. Would you share that story of deal making and brainstorming from your Yahoo! days?

Tim: It actually traces all the way back to when I was at Broadcast.com. Basically what happened is we got a new sales VP who came in and he'd been with a variety of different startups which had gone from zero to a billion dollars. He knew that the problem for most of this is that we're so underfunded in the startup, we just try to do everything on our own, right? He taught me in a meeting, if you want to be successful, you've got to learn how to never go down alone. That when you get stuck in a situation, say trying to raise money, trying to make a sale, whatever. He says "Build a team." What he taught me is the difference between a tall team and a wide team. A tall team is a team of people who work in line with each other all the time. In the business world, think of it like sales manager, sales person, account coordinator; those three, they work in a vertical line, right? A lot of times, that's who's collaborating to finish the sale.

Those teams aren't as successful as the wide variety of teams. For example, think of the account executive partnering with someone in the marketing department, partnering with someone in operations who actually delivers on the signed deal, and then partnering with someone in pricing, in the finance division. That's a wide team. Multiple disciplines coming together around an opportunity because they all have a stake in the outcome. The wide teams absolutely beat the tall teams in the market because when you bring together diversity, ideas bump into each other, perspectives collide together, and that's where innovation really happens.

When I went to Yahoo! after the acquisition, I specialized in creating wide teams to conquer business development challenges, whether it was trying to sell something, trying to buy a company, or looking to acquisition, trying to do partnerships. We worked a lot on rapid problem solving because I believe that the speed in which we solve all those little problems that lead to the done deal is our only competitive advantage. Rapid problem solving is how companies get great and stay great.

When you look in the world of startups, whether you're going to go back and look at Facebook, or Airbnb, or Uber, that's what those people did. They just cycled through the thousand little problems that were between vision and reality. They did it faster. Think about this in the world of startups. Facebook was faster at solving problems, whether they were technical problems or problems. They were faster than Myspace. Uber was faster than ZipCar, who was the big kid on the block when they first came on along. Airbnb was faster than HomeAway, who was also the industry leader when they came along. When you look at a lot of these real trophy case studies on startup world, what I see is not a brilliant invention but in fact, rapid problem solving culture. In every one of those three cases, they were merely improving on an existing product.

John: That's so great. We're going to talk about both of those ideas because when you give a pitch to an investor, one of the key slides is who's on your team? If a startup founder were smart enough to buy *Dealstorming* and quote from it, that they don't just have tall teams, even though they're lean, they have a wide team and that everybody in the company is part of the team, and part of the sales process to generate revenue. That would make an investor sit up and pay attention of "Oh, this person's created a culture that's a little bit different from other startups I'm talking to."

Tim: Let's talk about that for a second. You make a good point. I've built a couple of startups in my day. I fell for the romantic notion that the ultimate startup is two engineers. Have you ever heard that? I'm not an engineer, but I've had a startup where it was me and two engineers. Then, they added more engineers, and then we raised money, and added more engineers. What's wrong with that? You are basically an engineering stack and a non-engineering founder. That is not a wide team, okay? When you think about a startup, you need to have your core engineering team, but you need to make that add from marketing and sales. You need to make that add for operations, or it could be operations/finance. You need to make that add to have somebody that's dedicated to say, partnership development, or whatever. As an investor's able to look at a founder tree, and see that they've recruited the center, the forward, the point guard, the shooting guard, the power forward. They go, "Okay, that's a real team." Here's the issue. If all you do in startup world is put together the skill positions, the engineer, for example, that's the equivalent in the NBA world of having a team comprised of the five best point guards in the world, but that's all you've got. They won't even win half their games, and I don't care who you pick. So, that's a very good point.

John: You said another thing that I appreciate: "Rapid problem solving is a competitive advantage, because that's another key slide that investors look for on the pitch deck." Which is, what's your barrier to entry? If you can show the mindset, and be an example would even be better, of how you solve problems rapidly with a short story, again, boom! That sets you apart from all the other pitches they hear. Those two great points. Another thing you say that I love is, "Sales genius is a team sport."

Tim: Yes, so if you want to build a collaborative culture, you must dispel yourself and your people of the myth of genius that believes in the lone inventor, the one person. The one person who comes up with the idea, and on his or her own, changes the world. It is a romantic notion that is not true.

John: Well, that's a big myth buster, isn't it? So many people are wanting all the credit, or especially if you're a founder, you think you have to do it all by yourself, and all the weight of the world's on you. It can feel very lonely, but, if you start collaborating with other people, maybe even outside of your company to get other ideas and other perspectives, and ask for their advice, it suddenly frees up your creativity.

Tim: It does. Think about Steve Jobs. Imagine if he'd never worked with Steve Wozniak, never worked with Tony Fadell on the iPhone. Think about all the collaborations that Steve Jobs depended on to be the world changer he was. Another way to think about it is, from the invention community. I don't know if you know this, but "Thomas Edison" is essentially a brand that stands for more than a dozen people in a lab than for the individual we think of, the man with the light bulb moment. There was a guy named Thomas Edison; he certainly was a coach/figure head. His name went on the patent. In the scientific community, they typically always attribute an invention to one person. It makes it easier to market those articles, or those inventions. The reality is, over and over again, from Charles Darwin to Eli Whitney, none of them did it on their own. It's just a romantic notion. That's important. If you understand that a great innovation is a bunch of people on a bunch of ideas creating a soup. Then, somebody notices something in the soup, call it the alphabet soup, they notice a legible word, that's when it all happens. It doesn't happen unless we bring people together, so we have to believe that genius is a team sport. What I mean by this is genius is not in the person, genius is in the work. If we, as leaders and entrepreneurs, don't understand that, then we won't collaborate unless we have to. Collaboration is not the last resort; it is the first step that we take.

John: That's great, because that sets the whole tone for the culture of the company you're creating. One of the things I want to ask you about is what you're doing in *Dealstorming* with innovation templates. As you know, that's what everyone's looking for is the big idea that's going to change things, that's going to have a huge growth. How did you come up with a concept of an innovation template, and what's in it?

Tim: I started my professional career in quality circle management. Now, this goes back to the '80s. At the time, United States manufacturers were under fire by Japanese competitors who had learned this new quality management technique. It was called TQM. Basically, it was all about being able to trace a manufacturing defect down to the root cause and then using statistical process to design away from it. We had to catch up, but we had to learn that inspection. That's not how you determine quality and manage quality. You determine and manage quality by finding the root problem, and then collaborating your way into a statistical model to eliminate defects by design. Anyway, I started to use a couple of different techniques and then they worked for me again later in sales, and business development. I'll give you an example, John. In lean manufacturing in Japan, starting at

Toyota, there was a process called the "five whys"—what a manager would ask to get to the root cause of the defective product. Someone might say, "We are getting a lot of brakes returned because the left and the right don't match perfectly." That's a defect. That's a symptom. The manager might ask, "Okay, why is that?" "Well, because the lave at the factory doesn't cut them completely equally. They're only perfect ninety times out of a hundred. That's why we have ten percent defect." "Why is that?" Second why.

The person says, "Well, because they go slightly out of calibration over the course of several days. And, that's why, eventually, since we only calibrate one a week, that's what creates the variance." "Why is that?" "Well, we only do the calibration once a week because we have to bring in an outside company to do it, and we don't have the budget for that. So, we only have a budget for once a week." "Well, why is that?" "Well, because when we made the presentation in Japan about defects, they told us that that was an acceptable amount. And, that we have our budget for calibration, you know, based on that. But you know, obviously that's not right."

Then the last question is, "And why is that?" It's that, "Because Japan headquarters doesn't understand the cost of re-work. They don't realize that re-work is three times more than manufacturing, and there's the root cause." Now the manager says, "Oh, so the solution to this, cascading solution to all of this, is to create a cost of re-work down to the skew level." They're not just listening to some general number like ten percent. They're realizing that it's causing the factory to lose $250,000 a day. This changes everything. Now, "We will approve the cascades," right? Now, "We will approve calibration every single day to get rid of variants," and that's exactly how Japan conquered their quality problems.

This is the same for a business. When someone calls and says, "We can't get a term sheet from that VC," you back into it. You start out. "Why is that?" "Well, first of all we can't get them to call us back." "And why is that?" "Well, maybe when we presented to them, they kept asking about traction and we were explaining how it was, but we just don't have that many users, so we're really stuck on traction." "And why is that?" "Well, because this particular VC only invests in traction, they don't really invest in IP, or teams." "And why is that?" "Well, because this VC got burned three years ago by investing in a great team." Now you have your problem. You're going from "We can't get the term sheet signed" to "We have to help this VC get rid of this hangover." Or, "We have got to find a VC that does invest in people and ideas, not just traction." So, I'm using a startup-centric five whys, and that's a template. That's a really good template, because to quote John Dewey, "A problem well defined is half solved." What I found is that in many situations, we try to brainstorm before we know the root cause of the problem. So then we brainstorm a solution that reveals yet another problem, which frustrates us. It's like whack-a-mole, and you're the mole.

John: So you should wait to brainstorm until you really get to the root of the problem. That will save you tons of time and lots of frustration, right?

Tim: There's a saying that's been attributed to Abraham Lincoln: "If I had six hours to chop down a tree, I'd spend four hours sharpening my ax."

When you think about collaboration, please invest at least twenty-five percent of the time having an honest and transparent discussion about the root cause of the problem that has you there to begin with. Because, every deal is a hundred problems solved.

John: That's so true for an investor, and what the investors are looking for when they listen to a founder pitch them is, "How do you think? How did you come up with this idea? How did you get this team?" The fact that you could talk about how you solve problems rapidly to get this competitive advantage we talked about earlier through this innovation platform from the whys would really make your pitch stand out, wouldn't it?

Tim: If you're in front of an investor and you say, "We have a product that is going to appeal to a really big, addressable market. We think it's a outstanding, very fit competition to all the other existing products in the space. But what makes us different is that we have a culture in place of rapid collaboration. We've built a process that's scalable and repeatable that helps us bring people together when we get stuck anywhere—business development, product development—and rapidly solve problems. We benchmark solving problems faster that our nearest competitors." That's going to impress an investor because that speaks to maturity. When I've looked at some recent investments, my question is always, "Okay, give me a situation where you can get stuck on traction, whatever it is." Build a product, make a sale, acquire users, that's usually the three areas you get stuck in. "What do you do when you get stuck in acquire users? Talk to me about that process." If they look back at me and say something like, "Well, we'd try something new or we'd try it again." I reply,

"Well who is this 'we?'" If they point to the other guy and say, "Me and my partner," that is not collaboration. That is partnership. There's no diversity there. It's two point guards I'm staring at. That freaks me out.

I want to have them look back at me and say, "Well, that's part of why we want you to invest in us, because we want you to join our collaboration web, because this is what we do. When we get stuck, we talk to competitors, other startups that we've met at conferences who have this same problems, right? We talk to existing business partners like Rack Space and they help us. We're actually good at recruiting inside champions for the customer. But we collaborate, we have this process, and what we do is we pick a team of everybody that has a stake in the outcome, or expertise about the problem. Then, we write a deal brief, and they get the brief three days in advance. We have a two-hour meeting with the following structure. Then after the meeting, we have this execution process in place. And, we repeat and rinse until we solve it." That is really impressive to an investor because that's something that mature companies eventually figure out. The startups don't do it that way.

John: Right, and it's that emotional intelligence that you were speaking to earlier, and that's why investors love investing in serial entrepreneurs because hopefully they have figured that out. But the information you just gave somebody who is possibly starting their first startup, they can now save all that frustration and make themselves look like an experienced startup by just having that kind of answer and structures set in place.

Tim: I've always taught the four Ps of investing. Investors invest in past, meaning how many times have you exited. That's the big one, by the way. There's nothing in your bio descriptions that will sing more than got somebody's money back, or was on a team that had a big exit. So, there's past. The second P is people, and what that means is they can execute and build something. It's really important that when you talk about someone's bio, if they don't have a past of returning money or being part of an exit, they do have a past of building stuff, right? We don't care where you went to college. We really don't. We don't care what product you're associated with, or what great company you're associated with. We want to know what you've built, because when I talk to a lot of really good VCs, they're always asking, "Is that guy a salesman or is he a real builder?" So, when they look on a bio sheet, they're looking for people that can get work done with their money. That's the most important second P. The third P is product, and the fourth P is process. Process is what I like to call the human software of a company, like "this is the process by which we attract users. This is the process by which we build or improve products." They're looking for the Ps once again: past, people, product, and process, in that order.

John: I love that because the two reasons companies go out of business that are in startup mode is lack of funding and lack of customers. So, you, as the founder, have to make sure you have a good product market fit, or you get customers something they're willing to pay for. Then, you have to be able to sell yourself to get funding. You're selling yourself to get customers. What really makes *Dealstorming* the number one book that every startup should be reading is that it shows them the skills they're going to need for customers and fundraising.

Tim: That's right. You're going to need it over, and over again. Raising money is just the first hard deal. The other thing I'll say is, if you sell a service to a business, whatever the technology solution, an advertising solution, if you are business to business, you cannot social sell and test and scale, and be successful. This is the Millennial's dream, but it's not true. This is a big concern I have for startups. We live in a world today where they want to build a sales development rep model where they social sell to create contact. They use email to get you to try the demo. They give it away to you free. Then you eventually subscribe and then they scale up your subscriptions where it starts out at 5,000 a year with a dream of going to half million a year. Guys, that is not a sustainable business. Let me tell you why. A competitor who's got more courage to go after the million dollars in the first place, and put a human being in front of that buyer or buying team, they will eliminate all of the room for you on the deal. I can't tell you how many small startups are like, "We were inside Zappos, we were working with them for ten months, and we've gone to 500 users, and we're building 6100 a month. All of a sudden, this other startup came in and did a $700,000 deal, and everything's gone." I asked, "How long did it take them to do that?" "Two months. They showed the customer how much they could save by working with one solution provider, how much more efficiency they could get by getting reporting from one solution provider." So I said, "Well, the difference between you and them was they had the process and the courage to go after the whole deal, and you were stuck trying to do what I call the no-resistance model of startup sales."

John: Just give us a little sliver, let us prove to you this works, and there's no risk. But, the risk is somebody else is going to be brave enough, as you said, to come in and ask for the big enchilada, right?

Tim: We'd rather be ignored than rejected. That's why social selling's so hot. That's why email marketing is so much more fun. You'd much rather 'like' somebody's content, and then message them and say, "Hey, I've seen you do the thing. I'd like to have a quick webinar to show you our product." Then, you would email them a link to the demo. You never have a live conversation where they can basically say "no. I reject you and your product." We don't want to do the "live ask" anymore. The quality deal really is the only way that you build barriers to entry in the world we live in today. *Dealstorming* gives you a process, even when you're small, to build a quality team inside and outside your company, and conquer huge deals. I have worked with startups in the last few years that have had to go in and ask for two, three, four, five million and then ended up getting to avoid a B round by making a sale. If your B round was a couple of big deals instead of another beat down, or another dilution, I'm telling you, that's the way you want to do it. Too often, especially these startups, they just believe there's going to be a friends and family, there's going to be an angel, there's going to be an A, and a B, and a C. No, I say, pursue quality deals early enough with this *Dealstorming* process and A round might be your last.

John: I'm so excited for everybody to get *Dealstorming* in their hands because I know all your other books have been hugely successful, and this is going to be the biggest one yet.

Tim: Thank you so much, John. I appreciate you and what you are doing.

DAVID HOWITT
HEED YOUR CALL

David Howitt is the founder and CEO of the Meriwether Group and the author of **Heed Your Call.** In that book, he talks about the journey that founders take that's very similar to the journey of **The Wizard of Oz,** where you start your idea and you go from a black and white world to suddenly it's in color and everything is wonderful. Then you meet a witch who gives you some obstacles and that could be many different forms of customers not buying or there are more challenges than you thought, but you find some mentors along the way who go on the path with you, but you still have to walk your own path. Then you realize when you get to Oz that you still have to find all the answers inside yourself. The Meriwether Group has an accelerator program and people graduate from that and they invest capital and then the Group continues and helps them with an exit. In our conversation, he shares several examples of how he's done that.

John: You have quite an impressive background. You worked at Adidas, both in their legal division and then went to licensing, and then you and your wife launched Oregon Chai, which you sold successfully in 2004. There's a lot of the journey that you talk about in *Heed Your Call* about what made you find the courage to do what makes you happy. You now have the Meriwether Group, which helps founders through a variety of things that we'll get into. But first, can you provide a little context of what it was like when you were miserable as a lawyer and how you found the courage to leave that career path and start your business with your wife.

David: In terms of the law firm and my journey, I think like most of us, I sort of stepped into what Joseph Campbell refers to as the "known world." Campbell was the foremost authority on mythology who looked through a variety of cultures, spiritual belief systems, time, and geography and realized that there's one central mythology, one central myth that's been prevalent through all of those things which in of itself is powerful. In that myth, which he refers to as the "Hero's Journey," he built a road map, a kind of articulation of one person's journey in life. What I found in reading that is it's truly applicable to all of us and applicable to business. My known world was growing up in a middle class conservative town in Michigan and having parents and grandparents and neighbors and friends and teachers all of whom I listened to and respected and admired. All those voices had kind of a central thesis which is you should go do this and for me that "this" was you graduate from high school, you go to a four-year college and then you go on to some form of grad school, you graduate, you go get a great job somewhere that you may or may not like (you probably won't), but that has a high level of earning

potential, you meet someone, you get married, you have a couple of kids.
You buy a house and check all the boxes. I subscribed to that, and my known
world took me all the way to the point that I found myself in a very large law
firm. One day, I woke up and said, boy, I'm miserable. This is really not a
happy place for me. I don't feel like I'm in alignment with what is my truest
self and it's starting to show itself physically, emotionally, and spiritually, and
I need to think about what to do. Of course, at that moment, ego jumps
in and starts screaming at you, well, there's nothing you can do; people will
think you're insane if you quit this job. You'll go broke, you'll be homeless;
your wife will leave you, your neighbors will think you're mad. So, I struggled
with it for a while, probably close to a year, before I got to a place where I
finally decided to surrender and let go, because it had become so painful.

John: You talk in *Heed Your Call* about how we're so concerned about
worrying about what other people think about us and wanting acceptance
that we live our life from a place of fear and try to control things all the time.
I think everyone can relate to that, no matter where you are on the startup
journey. Whether it's your first startup or your fifth, there's a journey, and
overcoming fear is a big part of it.

David: In our society in business and in our personal lives, we're told that
fear or that letting go or surrender is the equivalent for failure, that it is sort
of waving the white flag and admitting defeat and being a failure.
But in Buddhism, it's exactly the opposite. One of my mentors and guides,
Deepak Chopra, who is very successful in business and in life, said, when
we surrender, when we finally let go, actually that's when possibility is at its

highest. That's when creativity is at its highest and that's where our ability to co-create a result in our business and in our lives is at its highest. It's by surrendering, it's by letting go that, in fact, we invite in the potential to actually align ourselves with our highest and best.

John: When we let go, possibility and creativity are invited in. That's a great insight.

David: What I want to say also, everything I try to put forward in *Heed Your Call* is stuff that I've seen illustrated in the world in business. So, I felt like there were a ton of great spiritual books out there and a ton of great books out there on business, but maybe not one that had built a bridge between the two. I thought, having grown up in a home where there wasn't a lot of spirituality around and having gone to law school, I should write a book that was grounded in actual business cases which show that the ego could let down a little. That concept of surrendering and letting go and allowing for creativity and for possibility is something I have seen demonstrated in many successful businesses, including Oregon Chai.

John: Yes, well one of the things that I really resonate with what you just said that's in your book is, "When we dial up too much of our left brain tendency and ignore our more empathic and intuitive nature, our relationship with the collective consciousness diminishes." I'm personally really fascinated with that, because what I do is I help the founders, tech founders in particular, who are very left brain about how something works. However, when they're pitching, what they don't realize is they have to move to the right side of the brain, which is the spirituality, the storytelling, the emotional engagement. That's where all the selling occurs. Let's jump right into one of my favorite stories in your book, about your grandfather. What an amazing influence he was on you.

David: My grandfather was not a traditionally educated man in the sense of Western culture. He didn't have a big college degree or grad school degree, but he was a successful entrepreneur and a very successful person, and he credited that with what he referred to as using common sense. When I dug a little deeper on what he meant by that, effectively what he started to articulate and I later really came to understand, is that comment that you mentioned about what you do, which is help people to toggle so seamlessly between the left brain and the right brain, which we refer to at the Meriwether Group as the power of 'and' that you need to have: you need analytics, but you also have to have artistry. You need to have intuition in addition to intelligence. Prophet spelled with a PH and profit spelled with an F; when we combine our whole brain, when we bring our truest and fullest self that the magic happens. With regard to my grandfather, I think he embodied that. You know, he had enough of sort of that left brain chops. He understood how to build a profit and loss statement, how to look at an income statement, margins, supply chain, the consumer. He probably wasn't the best at it, but he was certainly capable. He also had empathy and the ability to understand his consumer deeply. He got his audience and, as you suggested so well, when you're working with your clients you need to help them understand deeply. In *Heed Your Call,* I speak of deep empathy; our ability to be connected to the other is so present at any given moment. If we just allow ourselves for ego to quiet down, we truly can walk in another person's shoes, sit in their seat, truly appreciate and understand what it is that they're living with and/or looking for and then we can shape our message, we can shape our pitch, we can shape our business, our product, our service, in a way that's going to most likely be embraced by our audience, our consumers.

My grandfather talked about these subtle shifts that were really pretty powerful. The one you commented on, when you look at life and certainty in business, you're going to have multiple times, I certainly still do, where you're going to hit a wall, where you're going to have someone in the organization you're butting heads with, where we're going to have some type of challenge or hardship that is really in your face. I think for most of us when that happens, we go into this victim mentality of why is this happening, woe is me, this is so hard, why do I have to deal with this every day. But if you can shift that as my grandfather taught me and ask yourself, why is this happening for me? What is the lesson here? What is the mirror that is being held up to me that's going to allow myself to grow as a professional, as an individual, as a boss, as an employee? I think when we look at life through that lens, suddenly the shift allows us to actually approach these challenges through a lens of possibility instead of a lens of being restricted.

I think most of us think of a guide or a mentor as someone who is there to really help you, who is your friend, who is there to give you positive reinforcement and tools. Carlos Castaneda talks about guides and mentors who are actually there to create impediments for us. They're still your guides, still your mentors. They don't do it in a way that feels as good, maybe, but they're there to help us overcome elements of our personality or of our journey that are going to allow us to move further down the path. So, when you find that in your work, in your job, think of these people as a guide or a mentor and find what it is that they're there to teach you about yourself or the world.

John: There's so many things you said that I want to recap. First of all, I've never heard this phrase you said: Prophets with a PH versus profits with an F. With this prophets and profits, that is absolutely brilliant, because it's the whole 'and' philosophy. Your book talks about the need to be the thinker and the dreamer. You need to be the artist and the scientist. You need to have prophets and profits. Your analogy in the book is that even music has light and dark keys, and you need both sides to make that sing for the investors when you're pitching. I mean, it all ties together in such a great metaphor that you said. Thank you for that. Your book is broken into three different sections: initiation, mentors, and mastery. I want to touch briefly on each one of those sections. The initiation, the thing that really stands out for me is, you not only have to hear the call, but you have to *Heed the Call,* hence the title of the book. The mentors that you just touched on is the idea that most people just assume mentors are only going to be your cheerleader, if you will, and help you. What you just said is so interesting, that somebody might not have the label of guide or mentor, but if they're giving you a challenge, if you shift your perception, they can absolutely become a mentor and then, of course, the whole mastery. So, let's dive into mastery a little bit, which is what you do at Meriwether. Can you walk us through the different options that you provide founders from the accelerator to giving capital?

David: The Meriwether Group was really based on the power of "and" and based on being with an entrepreneur and a business owner through all facets of their journey. We can help you understand how to grow your business and actually be there to assist you with the work. We can add capital if that's necessary as part of your growth, and then when you've reached your defining moment, we can assist you through an exit that is high water mark economics. The old model was very disjointed, very disconnected; we do something entirely different. We add the right brain to that older model, back to Joseph Campbell and the Hero's Journey. I'll use an illustration to clarify. The Hero's Journey has been a central sort of thesis for many of the biggest movies and books. George Lucas cites Hero's Journey as the basis for Star Wars, for example, but I'm going to use The *Wizard of Oz* as a way to kind of explain what we do at the Meriwether Group and how it ties back to this notion of the Hero's Journey. We at the Meriwether group define the entrepreneur as the modern day hero. It's our belief that entrepreneurs are birthing new businesses, disrupting the status quo, looking at the world and asking themselves where has the consumer been deprived of innovation, of relevance, and of a really good choice, and then bringing that to the market. Those people are modern heroes, more so than politicians, more so than maybe even folks and NGOs. So, we want to be in service to that hero. We want to be a guide or a mentor to them.

You have this founder and they live in the known world. From me, it was growing up in Michigan. We talked about that, but for some of us that desire to listen, that quiet spot inside of us that tells us, hey, this isn't what you should be doing or this path isn't your highest and best. For some of us, we actually get to a place where we open ourselves up to listening to that voice and that voice is always there. It's always present, but we do things to try to quiet that voice because that voice is a voice of change and a voice of risk. Ego doesn't like that, so we employ tactics to try to keep that voice at bay and we say things to ourselves like, I could never follow my heart, I could never start this business, I could never do this. I have a mortgage, I have kids going to college, I have car payments, and as a result, we live our lives in the known world and we don't ever take that shot. You know, as an aside, in writing *Heed Your Call,* I spoke with a number of end-of-life caregivers and mostly those providing hospice care. They told me that the single biggest regret people have as they're reaching the end of their life is that they phoned it in. They didn't take their shot. That's where the regret comes in. Back to The *Wizard of Oz.* So you've got Dorothy and she's living in Kansas, that's her known world. She feels like there's got to be something more than a dirt farm in Kansas. She finds herself leaving her known world, and we all know she ends up in Oz, so this is the founder leaving their job, leaving their career, leaving the vestige to the known world and taking the leap and starting the company. Initially it's pretty euphoric: beautiful colors, people singing for her. She's excited, she's left the bonds of the known world and we all know this as business owners, we know this moment and we celebrate it, but it's pretty short lived. Soon, your "witch" shows up in a puff of green smoke and says, "I'm going to get you, my pretty."

Now, for the business owner that might be, well, this business idea is cool, but I didn't think through the supply chain or how I was going to market or is there enough margin or can this product actually be made, whatever.

You fall into what Campbell refers to as the abyss, that moment of despair where we have to actually surrender and let go. We have to give up, kind of drop our arms and say, you know what, I give up. I don't know that I can do this and interestingly, it's that moment in time when the mentors and guides show up and the reason is, I think, that before that moment of humbling, you're not going to be open to the advice or counsel of people around you, because you know it all, because you just started your business, you're all that. The Buddhists say that when the student is ready the teacher appears. And so it's this moment of surrender where we are now truly open to possibility and that's when people show up.

John: Most investors are constantly telling me we need to work with people who are coachable. So when you're telling this story, they must be humbled to surrender and become coachable, possibly for the first time.

David: Coachable, open to advice, self-aware, they know what they know, but they're also very aware enough to acknowledge what they don't know and where they need help. We will not consider working with or investing in a company until the founder has been at that point and so at that point your Obi Wans, your Yodas, and in this case, the case of Dorothy, your Lion and your Scarecrow and your Tin Man show up and they're there to walk the path with you. They can't take the journey for you, but they're going to be on the yellow brick road, alongside you on your journey; they're going to help you to learn what Campbell refers to as the tools of transformation. For our clients, some of those tools of transformation are going to be finance, operations, sales, marketing, go to market strategy, licensing, business development.

So, these are what we at the Meriwether Group bring to our clients when they're in that process of transforming the businesses where the founder and the owner are deeply on their path of growth. So, you're walking down your path, you're on your journey, you're learning the tools of transformation and now you reach your defining moment. For Dorothy her defining moment, she thought, was going to see the great and all powerful wizard. She had this notion that the journey was going to be something outside of herself, and of course, we know the story. She gets there and there is no great and all powerful wizard, and initially she's destroyed. What is this journey all been about? And one of her guides and mentors, Glenda, the good witch, says silly girl, all you have to do is click your heels together three times.

You've always had the power. You're the hero of your own journey. You are capable of doing whatever it is you want to do when you're in alignment with your truth, and that is truth of all the businesses we've worked with. They feel like that defining moment be something outside of themselves, but ultimately it is about them getting to a place where they're finally in flow and that may mean that it's an exit, a sale of the company, it may be an IPO, it may be an ESOP or succession plan or it may be bringing some executives into the leadership team that allows that founder to start thinking about their next journey. But it's true, because of the journey, the world is better and you are better for having taken it. For us at the Meriwether Group, the three main places on the journey are we where can help you build the strategy and help you actually execute on that strategy as a group of former founders. As a group of former business owners and entrepreneurs, we have walked the path, so now we'll walk it with you.

We can assist you with capital if that's one of the tools that you need along the path of growth. If you need capital, we'll make it available.

John: All that being said, let me ask you: what do you look for in a pitch?

David: As a person on my own journey, I'm not entirely interested in just being an investor. For me, I derive a lot of personal satisfaction from being part of the journey and it's just, okay, we need a check and thank you we'll be on our way. There are times we'll do that, but it's pretty rare. It's usually that we're working with you, we're in the journey, we're part of it and hey, we identified together you need x amount of dollars to really get to the defining moment, and we can make that available. Having said that, to answer your question, I think a few things are really important in a pitch, especially in terms of the left brain, right brain cooperation. We want to see that you clearly understand the business and you can speak to the financials, you can speak to a plan and articulate the critical components of how you're going to reach the plan. We want to see that as a founder and/or your team, that you have enough self-awareness to know that they're going to probably be areas where you're going to need help and be aware of those areas, be humble and not pretend that you know everything. We also want to see that the business product or service is disruptive, which we define either as creating a new category or one has not existed or looking at categories that are tired and complacent and are in need of evolution or revolution. I'll give you an example: Oregon Chai. There wasn't a chai category. There was tea, which was a mug of hot water and a bag of chamomile or Earl Grey. That's all there was. No one had created a new way to consume tea that maybe gave the consumer an experience that was a bit more like a latte or a cappuccino. We had this dynamic prior to chai where you'd walk into a Starbucks or a cafe and your choices were to have a really fun frilly sort of aspirational, experiential coffee drink or get a mug of hot water and a bag of the same stuff that my great-grandmother used dipped into her hot water. We wanted to change that. We redefined the drink, we were disruptive by looking at categories that were tired and stale, and changing that.

John: I want to acknowledge your wife's role with you in Oregon Chai, because in the book you talk about it so much and it was her passion and her tenacity that kept you believing, even when you didn't believe. The other key here is that when you're pitching, you must have the passion and tenacity that you're the people, and you must hold on that dream.

David: It's a great point. Heather was the right brain and I was the left and, unknowingly, we sort of came together. Whether you have a partner or whether it's just you, in any pitch, make sure you have equal parts passion and equal parts presentation. It's truly like having a child, and Heather was that incarnation and every one of the best pitches that we've seen that has been successful, every great brand and business has had an incredibly strong founder who has imprinted their DNA on a company, people like Phil Knight at Nike, Steve Jobs at Apple, these different people who gave birth to these companies. One of our favorite clients is Dave Dahl's Killer Bread. This guy spent fifteen years in prison and came out and decided he was going to launch a bread company. He looked at the category bread and, pun intended, it was stale. There was brown bread in the same wrapper, nothing differentiating them, so he created a brand that cut through the noise and as a result, he went from Portland Farmer's market to having sold his business for $275 million dollars.

John: What a success story. Congratulations. I know I saw that he's on your website as one of your clients. You guys helped make that story come true. It's not him by himself, but with equal parts passion and presentation.

David: I think you must have both. We want to see both in a pitch to us. You know, if you're too left brain and you're just super buttoned up on that stuff, it's not going to capture our attention because there is nothing about it that is aspirational, there's no passion in it and you're going to be a company selling widgets. If you're too right brain and you have all the beauty and all the meaning and purpose and all of the storytelling, you're an art gallery or a non-profit and that's wonderful, but we're not going to be interested. It's when you combine the two that's where the magic happens.

I mean, interestingly, Google is hiring more MFAs than they are MBAs right now. I have worked a lot with Nike; their senior executive team tells us they're not a company that sells shoes and apparel. They're a company that shares experiences and, oh, by the way, we have this product that you can use. I think those pitches, businesses, and business owners that know how to encapsulate that are successful. How can you be beauty and art and also be profitable and scalable? You know, how can you have passion and also have P&L and when you can braid those together, you are going to create something that the consumer is going to yearn for.

John: Yes. Beautify said. David, is there one book besides *Heed Your Call* that you would recommend to founders to read about investment?

David: Can I answer with two books? I referenced a bunch of times in this conversation and in our discussion Joseph Campbell, but I think there's so much in there that can be helpful to a founder and learning about themselves, their business, and that's Campbell's *The Hero with a Thousand Faces*. The other book is *Siddhartha* by Hermann Hesse. It's not a quick read, but again, I think there are so many takeaways in terms of how you approach life and business that can be really powerful for a business owner and founder.

John: Fantastic. We're so honored to learn your life lessons not only by what it takes to be successful, but this huge takeaway of prophets and profits, the thinker and the dreamer, the artist and the science. You are someone who walks your talk. I admire that so much.

TODD HERMAN
BE AN OLYMPIC STARTUP

Todd Herman is someone who has the Spanish royal family
and billionaires as clients. He sold and exited successfully from two
businesses and now has an incredible Ninety Day Year program for
entrepreneurs. He's also a coach for professional and Olympic athletes,
and he compares being an Olympic athlete to being an entrepreneur.
He won the top salesperson of the world in 2010 at the International Ad
Festival. He has a lot to say about winning pitches.

John: Todd, I love that you are such an expert on what it takes to become an Olympian or professional athlete.

Todd: There was a study that just came out a little while ago that my wife shared with me. It's all about risk tolerance, and they found that of groups of people that are out there, no two groups have a higher threshold for risk tolerance than entrepreneurs and athletes. It's funny, because I think the threshold tolerance was like 79-82%, something like that. Generals in the military are the only group that actually rate slightly higher than they do. Everyone uses the word "potential," and in my world, in my business, that word is not allowed to be used because I don't believe in potential. I think of potential as a crutch that a lot of people like to lean on to basically excuse away a lot of their bad habits or poor behaviors. What I look at, and the other thing really an investor is going to look at as well when they're taking a look at a successful pitch is, okay, even if you watch on "Shark Tank," people may like the grand idea that you have there. That would be considered potential, but what's the real performance? Tell me the numbers. Even with athletes, I want to know, what are your numbers? Don't tell me about what you think you can do. I want to know what's showing up on the court, on the field of play. The great thing about dancing between these roles of athletes and entrepreneurs is they're both manic people. You've got crazy ideas to think that you could actually go out there and somehow be the number one sprinter in the world or that you could somehow go into a meeting and walk out with five million dollars for this idea that started rattling around in your head months or years ago. These are crazy people, but I love working with them.

John: Well, I really like what you said there about the idea that what you have for your product is your potential, but what really counts is your ability to execute that idea. What are your numbers? Todd, you've had two successful businesses with great exits. So, you clearly have been down this path, but I want to go back even further. I watched a short video you did about a life lesson you learned from your father. Can you talk about that?

Todd: I grew up on a farming ranch in Western Canada. I live in New York City now, but I'm still at my core a farm kid. Once, in New York, we were walking out of a steak restaurant, I had some meat stuck between my teeth, so I took a toothpick and when I walked out the door, I tore it out of the cellophane, which I tossed to the sidewalk. Dad stopped, walked back, grabbed the cellophane and stuffed it in his pocket and kept on walking. I thought to myself, that is a perfect example of how you win at life, by taking care of all the little things. He didn't make a big deal of it, but he did it. Most people always focus on the big stuff, but my experience in working with high performing people is they are fanatical about making sure the details are well taken care of. I'm friends with Brian Fetherstonhaugh, the CEO of Ogilvyone, one of the greatest advertising agencies on the planet. We were doing a presentation together and the gentlemen who put together the slide deck had come in. Then, his assistant and I watched as Brian went through that presentation, picking out little punctuations errors or the little alignment issues. He's the CEO. Most people would think that they wouldn't care about those things, but someone who is operating at a high level does care about that impression, because, just like the best people have a tremendous eye for detail, these people are highly successful. So, the analogy is just take care of the cellophane in your life, because it matters.

John: It does. I love that you brought that up about the details on the slide, because I've had investors tell me, if you have a typo on your pitch deck, that's it. That's a no right off the get go, but what I love so much about that story about your father is that it shows that you're a master storyteller. I'm constantly working with my clients to teach them how to become a master storyteller. You described how old you were. You described that your father didn't make a big deal of it, but you took his lesson and continue to teach other people. If you want to win at life, take care of the little things. There are so many things of take care of, but the little things do matter, and you demonstrated how to be a storyteller. Now, I want to hear about how you won greatest salesperson in France, because, let's face it, when you're pitching, you're selling yourself and your idea to investors, so there must be a great story there.

Todd: Well, that's actually how I got involved with Ogilvyone, because Ogilvyone and YouTube teamed up in early 2010 to do this search for the world's greatest salesperson. The prize was going to be a fellowship at Ogilvyone. I wasn't really doing it to get a fellowship at Ogilvyone, but how I found out about it was a good friend of mine sent me a tweet to let me know about the contest. He knew that David Ogilvy's book Ogilvy on Advertising is one of the first books I give people when it comes to just learning how to communicate or sell or market yourself. My friend said, they're doing this cool thing, I think you could win this, so I went and saw their tongue in cheek launch video for it. What they asked people to do was to submit a two-minute video of how you would sell a red brick on YouTube. As soon as I saw their pitch video, I was like, well, I know exactly how I'd sell that red brick. I was working on an important project at the time and I was like, you know what, I'll get to this later, which I teach all my clients is famous last words, because you will never get to it later. If you're inspired to do it and it's something that's really going to make an impact, do it now. So, I did some self-coaching there, got up quickly, threw on a sports coat, wrote a short script, and an hour later I had the video done, in the can, and uploaded to YouTube. My whole shtick with the red brick was that the red brick was used to help build empires, because the Samaritans who invented the red brick used it to build pyramids. It was also used to build roads to help connect us all, because bricks were originally the thing that we used on roads, and then ultimately red bricks helped to revolutionize homes. They were no longer vulnerable to whims of nature, but at the end of the day, all of those innovations started in the mind of one person and just like them, you probably have an idea, a dream, a goal or something that you have never taken action on, so if you buy this red brick, it will be a message not only you but the world around you that you've laid your first red brick. You've taken your first step to a life of commitment action.

So, it kind of went on from there and then I said, you know, if you buy this brick, we'll donate the proceeds to the Red Cross earthquake relief effort in Haiti. Metaphorically, it would help to rebuild a nation. That submission video got me down to a final three, and the final three of us then were flown over to Cannes to the International Advertising Festival. I got a free trip out of it already. There was a gentleman who was like a Hollywood producer, and then a woman from Japan. We all had to do a short pitch about how we would sell the new Motorola Droid cell phone. Motorola was a client of Ogilvy and now we were in the biggest theater in all of Cannes, home of the Cannes International Film Festival, and we're on stage, and we've got two minutes. I had never been to an advertising festival. I had no idea what to expect, what the demographic of the audience was going to be there, so I actually prepared five different pitches based on different demographics. When I got there, I realized after meeting with many of the people that there was going to be a big chunk of the audience who didn't speak English at all. So, I thought, all they're going to hear is like wah wah wah, but I had my pitches prepared, so I thought to myself, okay, well, what is a character, a story, something, that when I say the word, it's the same word across every single culture. I was playing with the idea of, okay, Motorola Droid, just the word Droid is a cool cell phone. It's a technologically advanced thing, who would use that? Batman would use it.

I started off my pitch with, if you had the opportunity to design your own mobile device, the Motorola Droid cell phone would be that device. In fact, it would be the device used by Batman. As soon as I said the word Batman, there was this crowd of Greek advertisers in front, and I saw this one woman nudge one of her counterparts and she said, this guy is good and that's when I kind of knew I had the audience pretty well, but there was like, 1,300 people in the audience. Then at the end of it, everyone did live text message voting, and then the result was I ended up winning this and it was a great experience. Later, I met Mark Zuckerberg at the Facebook party. He came up to me and said, hey, aren't you the world's greatest salesperson?

John: What a great title.

Todd: It went on from there, and that's how I ended up doing a bunch of work with Ogilvy.

John: I thought there was probably a good story there, but you gave us two good stories. I love it. You know what, it's so interesting. I tell my clients, when you tell a story, give three points for people to take away and you said, if you have a dream, an idea, or a goal, right, and it just flows so effortlessly out of your mouth, but clearly you thought that out. So, people are going to say, I have one of those three things, so this is for me and that's so important when you're pitching. I work with my clients and constantly remind them that they cannot wing their pitch to investors. You had five different pitches ready, depending on who the audience turned out to be, and the key to success is knowing your audience. Investors are not all the same. You have to customize your pitch to what their specialty is and what their hot buttons are and what they like to invest in, and you nailed that and on your feet no less. You became the Batman and won the award. What a great story! So much great information there on how to pitch and how to connect with the audience.

Todd: To your point, I mean, there's a reason why rules of three are influential. It's the whole see no evil, hear no evil, speak no evil. Everyone knows, as soon as you say, see no evil, everyone else can repeat the next two things. So, you're right, organizing information into threes is exceptionally helpful to the audience.

John: Now, the Batman thing leads directly into one of your key areas of expertise, which is creating an alter ego. Can you speak to that?

Todd: The first business I started was doing mental game coaching with athletes, they weren't pro athletes at the time, because I was just out of school. I was young, but it didn't take long before I started working with professional and Olympic athletes, and how I got my name was I built up my name as being the person to go to in order to build a secret identity or alter ego to boost performance. This came about because I was an athlete. I was a nationally ranked badminton player. One of the devices that I used for my mental game was not going out on the field of play as myself because Todd has had his insecurities and his worries and his concerns about other people judging him, but that's not going to serve me on the field of play where I need to perform. What most athletes do, which is what they get wrong, is go on to the field and carry themselves with them as opposed to stepping into someone else who's going to perform for them. Actors do it. They go out on the stage and act as a character in order to deliver the results or the emotional response to the audience that makes the story believable. Well, if you want to make your performance believable, why not step into it as someone or something else, so I had this five-step process. I'm in the midst of writing the book on it. I've been doing this for well over a decade with clients, and I've started doing a lot more work with people in the corporate world or entrepreneurs.

I mean, there's a field of play that everyone steps on. When you go into a pitch, that right there is a certain rule, and there's a certain framework on how to be successful in that field or in that room. Yes, the idea is important and the numbers behind it important, but they're still investing in the entrepreneur, because you and I both know the odds of the thing that's being presented actually being fully the thing that shows up in the marketplace is, I mean, I've never seen that happen personally, and I invest in products and companies all the time. Ultimately, we're investing in whether I believe that this person can actually steward this thing to completion. Can they execute, or are they just an idea person who gets excited about something and then drops off three months later and now my money is gone.

Building out this idea of stepping into a better, heightened version of yourself on that field is the fastest way I've ever found to help people boost performance and get the result that they're looking for on the field. If you think about it, this is not about being fake, this is not about being unnatural; you are already doing it. In my case, I've got two little girls under the age of three. I am very different with them than I am as the hard-charging Todd, the coaching adviser that I am at work. So, who I am in business is very different than who I am in the home with the family, and then who I am with my friends when I'm out for a drink or watching the game is still another version of my personality just magnified to kind of accommodate that experience and so it's just that. When you get this, you become far more intentional and deliberate about who it is that you're creating, so that you can perform at the level that would be considered the highest levels, and then you get the result that you want.

John: I'm so glad that you said that, because I was going to ask you how you have an alter ego and still stay authentic. When you have a heightened version of yourself, that boosts performance. That is magic. That is gold. That allows you to still be yourself and somehow be better than yourself.

Todd: The word "authenticity" is a very big kind of buzz word that's out there even nowadays and I challenge people about it all the time. Here's my premise: I don't think anyone on this planet is really "authentic," because if people were authentic, the most authentic moment of your life was when you came out of the womb and you were bloody and you were crying. We all get our personality shaped, yes, after definitely being a father of two little girls, I can assure you that there are just things into their DNA. My wife Valerie and I have had nothing to do with shaping them in certain ways; it's just in them and you can't explain it, but there are environmental impacts, social impacts, there is the way that the friends we have help to shape our personality. So where does their authenticity begin and who they're showing up in life as that personality begin as well? My challenge to people is that I just don't believe in the word authenticity. What I care about is performance. If you're a good person to me, I don't know care if you're not being authentic in the moment. You're just nice to me. What do I care if you're being authentic? I mean here we are; I can say that the result was my interaction with you, John, was a good experience. So whether you were faking it or not, I don't really care.

John: The other thing that you're really on that I find so fascinating and useful is this whole concept of positive thinking versus positive expectations. In Silicon Valley and the startup world, there's this whole thing called the trough of despair that all startups go through. As you know, high performers tend to battle depressive states more than other people. Can you talk about that and what causes that and how can we handle those depressive states?

Todd: I think of life as having two classes of fish in the sea. There are the ones that live at the very bottom. It's cold down there, it's dark, light doesn't travel down to that level, and there is an exceptional amount of pressure down there. Now, currents can come along and maybe the fish that's living down there gets caught in the current and slowly that current starts to bring them to the surface, and if that fish doesn't escape the current and travel back down to where its natural environment is, they'll get eaten by a predator at that level or eventually get to the surface and the sun will burn them or whatever the case may be. They're built to be done there. Then there's another class of fish that's at the surface of the ocean; they're colorful and they're bright and they jump and they dance at the very top. If they get caught in the current and get taken down to the very bottom, they die because of the pressure that's down there. In my experience of working with thousands upon thousands of high performers at the Olympic level or entrepreneurs, whether it's billionaires or whatever, they're the people who live at the bottom of the ocean. They can handle the pressure. They can handle the intensity of what's it's like to be in these situations, and so I think the real problem that people are experiencing is that there has been this one rule that's set up in life that is life is about being happy and joyful, but I don't think that's accurate. I don't think that Elon Musk's sole purpose in life is to be happy. He has said that he is here to solve really big problems for this planet. You don't give really big problems to someone whose lens on life is to have just a fantastic lifestyle. I think that people need to be careful about the rules that they're setting up in their head and making themselves feel bad because they don't feel like they're happy all the time, because they're in a stressed out state. No, you chose it, or maybe it chose you. You're meant to do this because you can handle it. I've said that to some entrepreneurs and friends who have struggled with it and one of them remarked back to me, I've been living in just a state of worry and self-judgment for fifteen years. He sent me an email the day after. He's like, I have never felt more free than that. You just lifted so much pain and anxiety and self-judgment off my shoulders, because I felt I was doing something wrong in life, because I wasn't that typically very happy person. Now he's able to handle those depressive states. Now, I'm not saying that depression isn't an okay thing, but it is something that people who do big things deal with, because our roller coasters are a hell of a lot steeper, which means they're steep on the climb and that means the very top can be incredible, but they're steep as well and they can go a lot deeper than other people who just aren't taking on these kinds of challenge. So, the trough of despair is something that is very common, but the idea that you're a bad person for experiencing it isn't true; it's just the nature of the world that you're living. You are sort of meant to handle it and it's okay.

John: As a former swimmer, I love the analogy of the different levels of the water and I almost want to combine your two metaphors and say, if my alter ego is going to be a deep sea diver, I'm going to put on my deep sea equipment as my alter ego, so that when I have that on, I know I can handle the pressure. I won't always stay down there. I'll come up for air when I need to, but when I need to get the job done, I'm going to be able to handle the pressure. It's really helpful.

Todd: If I'm going to give someone a tool, that's it: that they can put it on and wear it to help them manage that deep level of pressure that we go through. So the first thing I try to get all my private clients to do is get into meditation. That is what ten of the top thirteen private equity traders in Wall Street. A major reason that they outperform everyone else is that they meditate every single day and that helps them avoid the emotional highs and lows that everyone else in the market is going through, because really what meditation does it flexes the frontal lobe. The frontal lobe of our brain is the part that allows us to stay focused, to concentrate and to mitigate the limbic emotionally part of our system. Studies have shown even if you do two minutes of meditation, it will help manage emotional states. People have a misconception about meditation; they think, yeah, I've tried meditation and I can't get my mind to shut off. Meditation has nothing to do with your thoughts going away. That's the myth that's out there. Meditation is all about being okay with what's passing through your mind and not getting attached to it. So, if you think about it this way, to use a metaphor: your mind is the sky, the thoughts passing through it are clouds. What most people do is they get some sort of self-judgment cloud passing through and they get entangled with the cloud thinking that's who they are, but I'm telling you, no, it's not, and here's the thing, we all think those thoughts. I've worked with the ultra high performers on the planet, so I can tell you they deal with those self-defeating thoughts too sometimes, they just don't get entangled in it and they continue to execute and take action.

John: Mediation is like clouds going through your head, just say next, next, next, don't get entangled in anyone that would bring you down, just go next. Keep the wind going, keep the clouds going, and I think that's so helpful, because like you said, so many people are so afraid and say, "I can't stop my thoughts." The goal is not to get stuck on one thought and keep going over and over it. How many times have we all done that?

Todd: Think about when you're just looking at the sky anyway. Sometimes you're just looking at clouds and you're like, oh, that's an interesting shape. So, the same thinking can go with your thoughts. You're like, oh, that's interesting that thought entered my head. Be more curious about it. Don't get entangled into it as that's me, that's who I am. It's more like, that's an interesting thought. How about that? What about that one over there? Try to be more of an observer of it rather than someone who is just identifying themselves with the thought.

John: I think that's the key is not being attached to any one outcome, especially when you go pitch an investor; you cannot be attached to that outcome, because they'll smell it and just like a date or anything else, you can't be attached. Is this the person that's giving me the money? Is this the person that's going to marry me? Is this, whatever, you just have to not be attached to anyone outcome, and you'll be at your top performance.

Todd: Staying engaged in the process. That's the key.

John: Are there any books that you want to recommend before we wrap up?

Todd: I think a great book that's out there, *Seeking Wisdom from Darwin* *to Munger* by Peter Bevelin. It is a fantastic book on just thinking in the context of models. Like, I'm a really big visual models person, and Warren Buffett has said that Charlie Munger is the fastest thirty-second thinker on the planet and that's because Charlie Munger has made it know that he has more than ninety different mental models that he's memorized from tons of different disciplines, whether it's mathematics or physics or literature or psychology so that he can think quickly. He doesn't get entangled in the whole subject matter. He goes, okay, what's that about? What is the idea of confirmation basis about so that when I'm listening to John give me a pitch and he's telling me why this thing is going to be successful, is he coming at it from a point of data or is it confirmation basis, because he's traveled down that road into this niche or this industry. So, he's able to think far more quickly and it's based in real data and real science. People think it may be really dry, but it's such a great book. Another great book that's out there—one that helped me with the red brick video— is called *Metaphorically Selling* by Anne Miller. She does a great job of giving examples of how one speech without a metaphor and one speech with a metaphor connects. I mean, you were talking before about stories. Metaphors are just a micro story, a sound bite for people. So, *Metaphorically Selling* is a great book and Miller is really smart.

John: Well, you've given us so many valuable insights into how to sell through metaphors, how to look at the numbers and not focus on your potential, not get stuck in your ideas, to get out of the trough of despair. Is there any one final piece of advice you want to give?

Todd: Continuously take action. That's it. That's just the hallmark of how you get yourself out of the trough of despair. Just keep moving, and do not define where you're at now with where you're going to be for the rest of your life. Keep taking action and you never know what's going to be around the next corner, you just don't.

John: Keep taking action. It's that simple.

JAY SAMIT
DISRUPT YOU

Jay Samit is the author of **Disrupt You!** He has raised over $800 million dollars in startups over the decades, and the foreword to his book was written by the founder of LinkedIn, so you can imagine how many people he knows and how many connections and insights he has on how to find an idea that disrupts things.

John: Can you take us back to how you first came up with the idea of getting into startups and what made you realize you really have a passion for that?

Jay: I'd like to say it was a plan, but I graduated as many Millennials did at the time of a great recession. You know, you did what you were told. You got good grades in high school, got into a good college, you did well in college and then bam, there's no jobs. So, back then it wasn't so easy to raise money, but I figured I would just go out and print a business card and suddenly claim to be a business, nobody would ever come and visit the business, and so I could morph and figure out what we did later. This way, my first company was called Jasmine Productions. Jasmine comes from my initials, JAS, Jay Alan Samit, and it was mine. From that humble beginning I happened to look at where new industries were happening, where could growth take place. The best message is that when we look out today, with all the changes in our world, I call this the era of endless innovation, where there's constant disruption. Well, disruption is either an obstacle or an opportunity, the choice is yours.

John: Your book says that you have to do three things: master personal transformation, seize opportunity, and thrive in this era of endless innovation. I want to start with this whole concept of mastering personal transformation. You talk a lot about that in your book about how important it is to think of yourself as a brand, first of all, and you have this great quote about how people are so interested in changing the world, but no one thinks of changing themselves. Can you speak to that?

Jay: Most of us by the time we get to be adults are carrying all this baggage of being told what we can't do. You weren't good at math, you can't read a map, you can't do this, you can't do that. For most people, they actually believed this, when in fact you can actually do whatever you want. If you really look at it that way and you stop saying what you can't do and start focusing what you can do, almost anything becomes possible. The most successful people in the world have the same twenty-four hours a day that you do.

John: Correct. You also talk in your book about the importance of just taking five minutes and visualizing your success and how important a positive attitude is to being successful.

Jay: Have you ever met or gotten a great idea from a negative person? Never. So, if you can just start your day by thinking about what's great, you are ahead of everybody else. Then, just start visualizing what you want to get out of the day, what you want to get out of life, what your goals are. If you don't know where you want to be in five years, you're not going to get there. So, your life is just like any other journey. You have to put out a map, what I call a disruptor's map, to really plan out. You don't have to know all the steps. That's where some people get lost in the process like, I really know that I want to direct Hollywood movies, you know, but I don't know what to do. Well, most likely, staying in Indiana is not the place to start. So, get yourself out of there.

John: I love how you say all disruption starts with introspection. That's such a key connecting element to your book about take a look at who you are, what

your strengths are, and what problem you can solve in the world.
As you say in your book, "Businesses don't sell products, they sell solutions."
Many startups that I work are in love with their idea, but they can't verbalize
to investors what solution it's fixing for people. You have done that time
and time again both for big companies like Sony and Universal, as well as
startups. Can you tell us about how you teach your students to look for
things that are disruptive and how that solves problems?

Jay: I've taken stakes in over eighty startups in my career, and investors
have made money almost all of those times. What attracts me—and what
anyone pitching needs to do—is articulate the classic elevator pitch, the
one sentence that explains what your business does. Tons of people want to
come to San Francisco for Mac World, but can't afford hotel rooms: Airbnb
just solved that problem, and so what is unique and where you can succeed
is you were the only person seeing the world from your point of view.
You are experiencing, every single day, problems and aggravation. Every
one of those is an opportunity, because if it's bothering you, it's obviously
bothering others, and the bigger the problem, the bigger the opportunity.
Becoming a global brand and solving a global problem is as easy as first
identifying it. So, just write them down. Write down three problems you
have every day. The beginning of the month it's pretty easy; by the end of
the month it gets tougher, but you have maybe ninety ideas, and then you
can work down that list and see which ones scale the most, which ones
can capture the value that you create. It's that easy.

John: That's such valuable takeaway, Jay. In your book, you write, "Problems are just businesses waiting for the right entrepreneur to unlock the value." You've certainty gave us an example of that with the Airbnb example. Another of my favorite takeaways in your book is with this concept you've come up with called the "zombie idea." Can you talk about that?

Jay: Everybody else tells you to nurture your idea, to grow your idea, to love your idea, and they're wrong. The best thing you can do with your big idea is kill it! Before you start hiring people, spending money, whatever, go to people in the field and find out why your idea sucks, why it'll fail, what's wrong with it. If you can start plugging those holes, you quickly discover that it wasn't such a good idea. If you go down that path and find an idea that can't be killed, that's your zombie idea. That's the one you start spending money on.

John: The zombie idea: everybody loves that concept that the idea is so great, the problem that it solves is so needed that it can't be killed. It's really a wonderful, clever way to get people to think about their ideas. So, we've talked about mastering your personal transformation. The second part of your book is all about seizing opportunities. You have one of the best stories I've ever heard about doing just that. Everyone has experienced a last minute cancellation or found out that the person is not able to see you right now, but you once had a brilliant solution to that obstacle.

Jay: If we go back about fifteen years, when the music industry was being disrupted, suddenly Napster comes out, everybody's stealing music, and the industry goes from a $40 billion industry to $20 billion dollar industry. Every sector is losing money, and nobody knows what the future is. As a serial disruptor, I want to change that industry and jump in with tons of ideas. I finally get a meeting with the CEO of EMI, the world's stand alone music company. This is the home of Frank Sinatra and The Beatles and Pink Floyd, everybody. The CEO is Ken Berry, who was Richard Branson's original business partner. I have this meeting, I show up at Capitol Records, go up to the top, the E floor. He's gracious enough to come out of his office and tell me that something has changed and he can't do our meeting. In fact, he needed to leave right away for the airport. Well, it's LA, so to get to the airport is at least forty-five minutes, so I said, "How about I just ride with you in the limo to the airport?" So, instead of getting a fifteen minute meeting, I got a forty-five minute meeting. During that time, I explained my visions and thoughts, I hear what his needs are, and while he's in the air, I now know for the next twelve hours nobody can reach him. I spend those twelve hours like a madman and write an entire business plan for what I believe the next five years of the music industry will look like. When he lands, that message is in his inbox. I got hired immediately.

John: Had you not seized that opportunity and been bold enough and creative enough to say, hey, why don't I ride in the limo and figure out your own way home from the airport, that would have never have happened. What a great example of seizing an opportunity. At another point, you had a chance to meet with President Bill Clinton at the White House. How did that come about?

Jay: I was very successful in the early days of launching what became the PC and the internet, which affected the way we see the world. One of the ways I wanted to give back is I had this vision we need to get computers into the schools. We need to get a computer to every class room. It's a very simple, but very big idea. I had no idea how to make that happen, but I would write about it and it would appear in magazines and I would speak at conferences. One day I'm sitting in my little software company, you know, there were twenty of us, nobody knows who we are and I get a call from the President of the United States. Of course I thought it was somebody doing an Arkansas accent pretending to be the President. To make a long story short, the White House believed in the idea and they invited a whole bunch of forward-thinking people together. We sat down and said, how do we make this happen? It was very inspiring. I mean, you're sitting in the White House, with the President, Vice President, all these really important people, and then they spring on you a new piece of information: there's no federal dollars to help you. We're there for moral support, but that's all it took. It just took people believing, and you got enough great minds together and the people that came out of this, it was amazing. I don't recall if it's in the book, but the fun out of this is we ended up wiring a school one day, a school in California for the press. It was more of a photo op than reality. Back then before WiFi, you literally had to wire, so the President is wearing a hard hat and the Vice President and at the end of it, there's photo op with the White House photographer. A month goes by, and I get this beautiful signed photo to me that's going to be framed to my wall forever, but it was a three shot. It was me, the President, and this other guy. I'm thought to myself, I really wish it was just the two of us. He's one of the guys in the committee that participated, you know, it's the kind of picture you want to show your mom. About ten years go by and a friend saw the photo and said, "You're friends with Eric Schmidt?" That third guy went on to become the founding Chairman of Google.

John: That's quite an accomplished group of people that you're working with. So, that whole concept is figuring out a way to solve a problem without a lot of money and everybody pooling their resources together, you never know who you're going to interact with. That's such an inspiring story.

Jay: Yeah, but the takeaway of the story is Eric Schmidt, who was a guy who just left Novell. He was looking for something new and meaningful to do. These people that become the legends of entrepreneurship, the disruptors that change our world, it didn't happen to them. It wasn't like, oh, I was walking down the street and I won a lottery ticket. They made it happen. They went out of their way. The majority of the world's billionaires are self-made. That is not something that existed in the past. This isn't about class, this isn't about race, and when I look at, you know, the big problems of the world, whether you go with climate change or water shortage or anything, the only people that are going to stop these problems are entrepreneurs.

John: One of the things you talk about is capital; you have a whole chapter about capital. A lot of entrepreneurs say, you know, I just need funding and then I'll be successful, and you have a whole creative strategy that you've used throughout your whole career called, "other people's money," OPM, without having to necessarily get an investor. One of the stories you talk about is how you got Sony Music, McDonald's, and United Airlines, which seem like completely separate industries to somehow work together and brainstorm something that allowed Sony Music to piggy back on their money. Can you explain that whole strategy?

Jay: Sure. So, you're starting a new business and it's aimed at solving a problem for some segment of the audience, whatever that may be. It might be elder care or maybe young people, maybe women, whatever it is. There are some other brands out there that also want to sell, reach, and work with that same target audience, and they have a non-competitive product. If you can figure out how to use their marketing dollars, their reach, their sales channel to promote what you do, then you're basically spending off-balance sheet financing. They're paying for you to become successful.

In the case of Sony, we were launching a competitor to iTunes and that was a big task to do. I was trying to figure out who else had problems. It doesn't matter what their problems were, but who else were in the headlines and one of the headlines at the same time was that United was coming out of bankruptcy and wanted to tell the world "come fly with United" and McDonald's had suffered through a movie called Super Size Me, which shows Morgan Spurlock nearly dying by eating McDonald's three times a day for thirty days. To make a long story short, I went to each of them with my idea. United said, we have all these people with frequent flyer miles that they're not using, what if we make it a currency that you can buy digital downloads with it, and McDonald's, what if we make you hip and cool by every time you buy a Big Mac, there's a free code on the box. It's called the Big Mac value track and you got a song. So, now you have McDonald's spending millions of dollars for great television commercials, putting signs in every store, bags, and all that, and then with United we did a concert in the sky with Sheryl Crow at 30,000 feet and filled the plane with press from Chicago to Los Angeles. It got the lead story on all the network news, all the newspapers, everybody covered it, and you now have millions of customers coming to your store, opening week, and it didn't cost you one little cent.

John: Let's not forget that you were competing against Apple's huge budget, so that is an amazing story about being creative and using other people's money, but people are willing to spend their money because you're solving their problem, in addition to having your own problem solved. I think that's the real genius behind what you did there.

Jay: If I could just build on that. When you pitch, it's the same concept. When I was in my twenties and pitching big companies, I would go in and say, oh, Intel, this will solve this for Intel, this will solve that for Intel. I thought it all out, everything. You know what? That's not what a pitch is. Pitches solve the problem for the human being across the desk. What motivates them? Are they trying to get a bonus? Are they trying to get a promotion? Are they trying to beat a certain competitor? Get in their mindset, because all you have to do is solve for the individual that you're pitching and all the rest will work itself out.

John: It's really having huge empathy skills, figuring out, what is their hot button? Is it that they need a promotion, that they need to hit a certain number? You also talk about it in *Disrupt You!* The truth is that a CEO is happy to buy your startup company if it's going to make them look good or help them solve a problem, right?

Jay: Large corporations are not set up to innovate. They're not set up to do that; that is our new thing to do. What they're busy doing is keeping what they've done, protecting it against gains from their competitors. They can't be paying attention to everything. So, for example, Kodak, competing with Fuji, misses the reality that people aren't using film any more, in the era of digital cameras. When the moment happens and you take those risks and you have that money-losing business for two or three years to prove your new concept, then it's at a point where they're willing to say, wow, we need to get in there. We don't mind overpaying, we don't mind buying Oculus Rift for billions of dollars though it doesn't have a penny in revenue, to take an extreme example. Even an incredibly innovative company like Google: they were late to the mobile market, but they bought Android; they didn't sit and create that on their own. You'll see this time and time again. Most of the millionaires that you think of who came out of Silicon Valley did so on businesses that were not profitable.

John: Just to expand on that concept of coming up with something that isn't necessarily hugely profitable out of the gate but still has extreme values for someone to want to buy, you also talk about how there are times where you do want to get investors to give you money for a percentage of your company. As you have said, 100% of nothing is nothing, whereas 50% of something can be worth millions and that you'd rather half the Pacific Ocean than all of Lake Erie. What a great visual that is. So many of our startups talk about valuation and, I don't want to give away too much of my company for this kind of investment, but like you said, 100% of nothing is nothing and if you need the money in order to make your company grow and scale and prove that it's viable, then 50% of something can be worth billions. I'd love to have more of your insights on that.

Jay: Sometimes I meet people who are afraid to give away something or they try to tell me they have a billion dollar company with no employees and no investors. You're not going to do it alone, so you better start figuring out that it is going to take a whole team of people, and you're going to be the Pied Piper leading them. In the beginning, your employees are going to have to come on that leap of faith; what's going to give them that leap is that they are going to get some of that upside, because they're going to be working for free or less than they could get at a job somewhere else. Your investors know that the vast majority of startups won't make it, so they're taking a huge risk, and so that's how it starts getting divided up. There's no other way. Now, there are clever ways to structure things and various ways to get into detail, too much to get into here, but I try to cover them in the book. In the basic premise, you want as strong as a team as you can. One of the things that sometimes people forget is that LinkedIn is a great tool for solving this issue. There are esteemed people in your field, in your industry, that you can just reach out to on LinkedIn, send them a note, and ask them for advice, and put up a group of advisers around your concept that will make you seem more connected, know the industry better, grow faster. That's an easy way and many of these people want to give back. It helps people feel validated that they're experienced, and that their expertise has made a difference.

John: You have some great ideas about team building; if you're recruiting somebody from a really big company, someone who has great skills and is in big demand, one of the ideas in your book that was so empowering and really made me stop was, "Would you rather work forty hours at a job you hate or eighty hours at work you love?"

Jay: I don't feel like I work. I mean, I put in a ton of hours, seven days a week. I don't golf, I don't sit around. I'm on a mission. When you feel like you're on a mission, there's nothing that's going to stop you. There's nothing more energizing and you sleep because the human body forces you to. I've been in, I don't know, maybe twenty cities in the past month. I fly around like crazy because the opportunity to help one more person, to change one person's life, to inspire one more person, it's selfish. It makes our world better.

John: What would you say your mission is? I mean, clearly, it's making a difference, encouraging other people to make a difference, right? Is that what moves you?

Jay: I truly believe that the people who solve world problems are entrepreneurs. We've got a lot of problems, and yet we don't teach people how to be great entrepreneurs. I'm on the wrong side of fifty; I grew up with *"I Love Lucy."* Lucy would have a get rich quick scheme, it would fall apart, and then Ricky would forgive her and life would go on. To today's generation, they grew up with *"The Simpsons."* Homer gets a crazy idea, it falls apart, and life goes on. That ethos is very specific to the American dream. The American dream isn't that anyone can get rich; it's that anyone can try. There is no fear in failure. Failure means that you tried. You learn more from failure than you do anything else. Bill Gates and Paul Allen had a company that failed. Did they get shunned? No. Their next business was Microsoft. Henry Ford went broke, as did Walt Disney. These are risk takers. You have to understand that failure is part of the process and not stop. You don't want to just give up.

John: And that brings up the whole concept of pivoting that you talk about in your book. That ability to say, this is what I think, I'm not afraid of failing, I'm going to get some feedback. I'm going to get some data; if that doesn't work, I'm going to pivot. You tell this amazing story of what YouTube originally had as an idea, and I don't know that many people know that. Would you tell us that story?

Jay: In the early days of internet dating, a couple of guys sat down and discussed the fact that internet dating just showed a still picture, which could be twenty years and twenty pounds ago. You should be able to know more about what that person is really like. They decided to make a dating site that has videos on it. So, they put up Tune In Hook Up as a video dating site, and they learned two things from the data. Nobody was really excited about dating any of these people, but tons of people liked watching the videos. So, they got rid of the dating part, put up more videos, and within a year changed the name to YouTube and became billionaires. So, had they not looked at the data, had they believed that their idea was so good and flawless and that they knew everything, they would have just gone their merry way out of business and never pivoted. Pivoting is a very hard to thing to do. You have to admit that you were wrong, but the good news is, you wouldn't have gotten to that point to get that data and see that insight had you not gone down that wrong path. So, going deep into the woods with your eyes closed, you're going to hit a tree and die. The whole point is to look at all this rich data that we get nowadays and see what your competitors don't have because they haven't gone through that experience.

John: I love that. That really is the third element of your book, which is thrive in this era of endless innovation by seeing the insights that no one else has seen. Sometimes that means the only way that you can see is by trying something that doesn't work. What a great, great book. Are there any other books you have your students read or anything you'd suggest for startups that are looking for either great ideas on pitching or getting investors to pick them?

Jay: I haven't seen one on how to raise money. There are good books on pitching, like *Pitch Anything* and books on how to make a lean startup or a tech startup. *The Lean Startup* has done very well, but what really drove me to write this *Disrupt You!* was the fact that I saw a lot of books written by journalists about what they think it should be, and then I saw a lot of books like the famous one by Jack Welch, one career, one moment in time, look how smart I am, but I really didn't see anybody that took the point of view of let's do a cross section of every industry and show how we all follow the same process, whether you're Richard Branson, whether you're starting LinkedIn, whether you're starting YouTube, any of these businesses or restaurants, or the many of hundreds of examples, Silly Putty to Odor Eaters, and I really wanted people to see not only how easy it is, but disruptions are not just about releasing value, but focusing where to capture that value. Shawn Fanning did a great job with Napster of disrupting the music industry, but Napster never captured any value that it unleashed. So, what's the point? It's really important to understand the complete value chain of a business and where those things go, so I tried to bring this in the most accessible manner. I hope that my ideas and my book help to inspire the next generation of entrepreneurs and innovators.

MICHAEL PARRISH DUDELL
"SHARK TANK" SUCCESS

Michael Parrish DuDell is the author of two "Shark Tank" books, **Shark Tank: Jump Start Your Business** and **Shark Tank: Secrets to Success.** He only had thirty days to write that first book. You can only imagine how much pressure that was. He was on the set. He knows all kinds of insights about what each shark is looking for when they hear a pitch. He says, "The key is just to be a human talking to another human. Be authentic, be transparent, and, of course, know your numbers." He shares what he learned from all that time in the tank with some of the best sharks in the business.

John: Before we get into the shark tank, let me ask you: how did you become a Millennial generation expert?

Michael: Well, it helps that I'm a Millennial myself. There are a lot of people out there who talk about the generation and who, maybe, speak on the generation, but who don't have that firsthand experience of being part of the generation. We know a lot about Millennials, but one of the things that we know is that Millennials learn best from other Millennials, and that Millennials prefer to be around Millennials. So, it just sort of helps that I'm of that generation. So, that's the short answer to a much longer answer, which is that in 2007, I became the Senior Editor of a site that's now been sold and changed a lot. But, back in 2007, when digital media was first becoming a force to be reckoned with, the conversation that we were having was a conversation with Millennials for Millennials, and that led to a lot of different kinds of work, to speaking, to writing, to consulting. It was quite accidental that, over the years, I turned into this Millennial expert and positioned right in the future of work in the small business space. There's actually a lot of overlap between some of the things we talk about in the book, some of the topics that I generally speak about, and this idea of the next generation who's going to be carrying the torch and taking over the future of business and entrepreneurship.

John: I don't think a lot of people realize that the Millennials are even bigger than the Baby Boomers, even though Boomers have the reputation of having changed everything, but there's more Millennials. Am I right about that?

Michael: You're exactly right. It turns out that Millennials are the largest generation in the history of the world. It was the Baby Boomers, but we have surpassed them. We're about eighty million members strong, and that means a lot. It means that we have an overwhelming ability to make purchasing decisions that affect numerous businesses. It means that when it comes to voting and when it comes to a lot of other activities, being part of that majority makes a difference. We're going to be leading the way. So, the conversation around Millennials and how Millennials grow and evolve into leaders and into adults is a fascinating conversation. I'm really honored to be a part of it.

John: Can you tell us about how you came across Seth Godin and what you did with him on the Domino Project?

Michael: Seth Godin is one of my all-time favorite people. I worked for him in 2011 as part of the Domino Project, which is a publishing company that Seth started. It was powered by Amazon.com. It's funny how we met. I share a literary agent with Josh Kaufman, who wrote the book, Personal MBA. Seth is also represented by our literary agent. In 2009, when I was twenty-five, I pitched a book to her, and she said, "Listen, there's no way I can sell this book, but I think you're interesting. Stay in touch." I did, and over the course of the years, we got to know each other very casually as acquaintances, and this opportunity happened. I saw on her Facebook page that Seth was looking for somebody for a project. I applied just like the thousand other people that did, and the rest is history.

John: What do you think it was about your application or your interview made Seth pick you out of all the people that wanted to work for him?

Michael: I don't know. That's a really good question. It wasn't a traditional "Submit your resume"; it was an essay question-based Google form that really required a lot of examination and a lot of personality in order to stand out. Like anybody who has cultivated their ability to lead and to manage and to run businesses, I think Seth probably has a good sense of the kind of people that he works really well with, and he can see through that sort of thing. Of course, it didn't hurt that I knew somebody who knew him. I think he just sort of knew. There was a whole interview process. I think there were close to a thousand applicants, and about thirteen of us were brought in for a group interview, and I believe six were chosen to work on the project.

John: Well, there are so many similarities there, Michael, to pitching to get funded, to pitching to get on "Shark Tank," the same kind of numbers. As you said, two things are key here: one, a warm introduction is always a great way to get in front of an investor, and two, you must show some personality. That's what people respond to, whether you're pitching to get hired, pitching to get funded, pitching to get on "Shark Tank," whatever. Do you agree with that?

Michael: Oh, absolutely. Listen, there are a million people with a million different ideas, and it all comes down to differentiation. The way that you differentiate yourself is by leading with your personality, by leading with that competitive advantage, which, for a lot of people, it's who they are.

John: Differentiate with your personality. So, how did you get from the Seth Godin connection to Amazon to getting selected to write the book for the "Shark Tank" show. I'm sure that was equally competitive.

Michael: There's a little bit of a gap between those years. After I worked for Seth, I went over to work as the editor of ecomagination.com right as GE was re-launching that property. It was a really great combination of all the things that I'd done in my career. I'd worked in the environmental movement in an editorial capacity, I'd worked in the business sector, I'd had this conversation with Millennials, and this sort of combined it all. Ecomagination was all about talking about the solutions to some of the rather large challenges we're facing from an environmental standpoint through the lens of business and how business can make a difference. I'm a big believer that business, probably even more than any other entity, is the one thing that can make a tremendous difference in this world. So, I was very proud to sort of help lead that up. Then, from there, I started my own firm, consulting and doing a lot of trainings and workshops all about things like media, content, Millennials, that world. And, through that, actually, it was a very random story, the same literary agent, who had connected me with Seth, she and I had met a few days before. I'd been looking for a book project, and randomly, she got a call from the editor at Hyperion, which has since been sold (now it's part of Disney). They said, "Listen, we're writing this book for 'Shark Tank.' We're looking for an up-and-coming entrepreneur and author who's familiar with the brand, who has experience in branded content to come in and write the book. It wouldn't be ghostwritten names on the cover, but instead the author would work directly with the sharks, do you have anyone who's interested?"

Now, there was a caveat. The caveat was that the entire book, from start to finish, had to be completed in thirty days. Of course, thirty days is an incredibly short amount of time to write a book. If you're doing the numbers on a 60,000 word book equals about 1950 words a day, every day without a break. So, a few writers were submitted. I don't know how many different agencies submitted. We had to do a few sample assignments. They chose me, and I went off to Florida to lock myself in a room and write the book. Not long ago we finished the second one, *Shark Tank: Secrets to Success*. So it did well. The first one is *Shark Tank: Jump Start Your Business*. The first one is very much a 101, how do you start tapping into some of the knowledge of the sharks and entrepreneurs. The second book picked up where the first one left off, and I traveled around the country with nine of the most successful entrepreneurs from the show. We told their stories from childhood all the way to where they are now, how they built their business, the trials and tribulations, and how, ultimately, they succeeded as entrepreneurs.

John: Fascinating. Were you actually on the set a lot?

Michael: I wasn't on set that much, but I was on a few times and got to be there during the filming of the fifth season, for some of those episodes. So, that was really cool.

John: What did you see is the biggest challenge people have when they make a pitch?

Michael: Well, you know, in that context, the biggest challenge, and perhaps it is the biggest challenge in general, but definitely in that context, it's the nerves, it's the fear of being in the spotlight— it's a very high stakes situation and if you're not used to being in front of the camera, that makes it even more terrifying. So, it's getting out there and really being afraid that you're going to be eaten alive by the sharks; in this case, the camera thing is scary and the world could possibly see it and you could mess up and all of that. I think that gets in the way most of the time. I think if you've made it all the way to the show, you have all the answers. You've done the research into what they're going to ask and you know about your business, hopefully. I think, most of the time, it's the fear that stands in the way.

John: Let's talk a bit more about that because it's a high stakes game whether you're on "Shark Tank" or in front of an angel group or a VC to deal with nerves. Do the people on "Shark Tank," the producers, require them to practice a lot before they start rolling the cameras to try to make sure they don't make a total fool of themselves?

Michael: They do get a practice around the day before and they've been up there. But they don't get a chance to do it in front of the sharks. What you see on television is the real deal. But, they have practiced it and over the course of the few months, usually, before they get there, via remote, they're working with the producers and folks from the show to nail down their pitch and make it something that is really enticing to the sharks. So, there is a good amount of coaching before they get up there.

John: Right. I've also read and heard that they have to stand there in front of the sharks for a few minutes while they set the lights, and the sharks automatically start judging them in terms of how comfortable are they in their skin before they even open their mouth.

Michael: It's pretty funny. It's the nature of television. You have to get the shots and ensure that there's to be some sort of production quality on top of all of that. So, there are some little things like that that, maybe, make it a less organic experience than one might think. I've read a lot, even from the sharks, about how long they're standing up there. I've read some people say, "Oh, they were up there for five minutes," and some people say, "Oh, ten seconds." When I was there, I would say, the average was about thirty to forty-five seconds, which is an awkward amount of time, but it's a part of the process and they know it's going to happen.

John: I just think that's still valuable for anyone who might be pitching because whether you're on "Shark Tank" or in front of an angel group, the minute you enter the building, leave your home, even, you are on. You've got to have your game face on. You can't just say, "I'm going to turn it on when I start speaking." You can't wait until you open your mouth. People start looking at you, how comfortable you are, how confident you are from the moment you walk into the room. I'm constantly telling clients, when you get a question from an investor or a shark, don't get defensive. Because the minute you get defensive, you're not coachable and they don't want to work with you.

Michael: Exactly. Look, when somebody is deciding whether to invest in a company, they're not just looking at what the business does, they're not just looking at the product or service, they're looking at the person and they're looking at the potential. Depending on the investor and their strategy and what's worked for them, they're probably putting weight on one of those categories more than the other. If you looked at the sharks on television, I can tell you right now, for someone like Barbara Corcoran, it's all about the person. She said this in the book and she says it time and time again: she will happily take a business that she doesn't think can make, yet, a product that's not going anywhere, turn it around, as long as the person is someone that she feels she can invest in. The person is honest, the person has integrity, the person's fun, and she wants to spend considerable time and energy with them. You look at someone like Lori Greiner: yes, she cares about the person, but she's a product investor. She really is looking at the potential of that product and how that product fits in the portfolio of what she does and of her other investments. So, it depends on the investor. The best piece of advice is to do as much research as possible, whether you're on "Shark Tank" or pitching at some sort of pitch competition, or even just having a meeting with an angel. Do as much research into who this person is, and into how they like to be approached, spoken to, and position your product accordingly.

John: It's all about the due diligence that you do on the investor as much as they're going to do on you.

Michael: I mean, we're getting into business with these people, so there is this idea that when somebody's approaching somebody for money, the power dynamic is, I'm asking you for something. That's totally wrong. You have to approach it as if you're giving somebody an opportunity to be a part of something that's going to make them money. This is with equal partnership. So, when I think about pitching, I don't like the idea of this subservient mindset where I really hope they give me a deal. Well it's 50-50. If you've done your job right, you're walking in with a business that has the potential to make these people a lot of money. You're offering them an opportunity.

John: That leads right into this fear of missing out that happens. I've had Charles Michael Yim on my podcast; he got all five sharks, pre-revenue, to put money in because they liked him and his idea so much, and they had this fear of missing out, "I want in. I want in." Do you see that often?

Michael: I think that's a valuable tactic, not just in pitching but across the board in business. We're taking risks all day. Nobody knows what's going to work and what's not going to work. We can make some assumptions about things based on previous situations, but at the end of the day, there's no proof that this formula or this plan is going to work. So, when you can position it in the right way and you can get people interested in what the potential could be, you can certainly help them with the idea that, if they miss out, this is going to be sort of a once in a lifetime thing.

John: I want to talk a bit about your second book, *Shark Tank: Secrets to Success.* Did you have more than thirty days to write it?

Michael: I had about ninety days, but it required a lot of flying and a lot of interviews. It was a very intense process. I think it works for the show because

I was put under a very tight timeline and very tough rules and regulations around writing the book, and doing it and turning it on deadline. I think that makes sense for the nature of the show because, really, the show is all about being an entrepreneur, and when you're an entrepreneur there's one thing that all entrepreneurial people have in common is that they get it done no matter what. A professional shows up, a professional does the work, and a professional doesn't miss deadlines. So, the books are very much an embodiment of that philosophy and an embodiment of the brand.

John: Now, can you share a story from Secrets to Success? I always love storytelling. I think that's the best way to communicate your message, and if you're talking about someone's childhood all the way through, it's always the why behind the why this particular idea to make their business, right?

Michael: There are so many great stories in there. I mean, I talked to some incredible founders and they've all gone through the process of starting a business probably so they have a lot of great stories. One that sticks out immediately is I spent some time with the brother and sister pair that put together the company Pipsnacks, which is famous for Pipcorn, which is the little mini-popcorn. One of the stories I really love from their experience is that when they were kids and they wanted to make some extra money. I think they were like maybe, 8 and 10. So, they had an air popper to make popcorn. They never had any idea that, twenty years from that day, they would be back in the popcorn business. But, as kids, they would make their own popcorn and go out in the street and they would sell it, and I just thought that's always really neat because when you see something like that, again, at that time, as a kid, you have no idea you're going to, one day, build a multi-million dollar popcorn company. But you see that the seeds are planted early and I just thought that was a really fascinating part of their adventure. But, there are lots of great stories like that in the book, so you got to check it out.

John: No pun intended, the seeds were planted early, right? The kernel — the idea planted in their childhood developed into something really, really wonderful. What is next for you, Michael? Are you going to be going on a speaking tour to promote Secrets to Success, or write another book?

Michael: That's a great question. Speaking is probably the biggest part of my business right now. I'm on the road, sometimes every week, sometimes every other week, but I'm doing a lot of speaking, a lot of training around this idea of helping business and leaders figure out what is coming for the next generation. What are some of the ways that they can really move forward and enter the future of work in a way that's going to work in the environment, that's going to attract the best people, the best consumers, the best employees? And a part of that is telling the story of "Shark Tank" and the story of the entrepreneurs that I've spoken with.

John: One of the key factors that investors look for, whether they're Barbara Corcoran or anybody, I think, is who's on your team besides you? So, if people can learn how to assemble a great team to execute their vision, that really is a big factor, not only as to whether they get funded, but whether you're successful or not. Are there any tips that you have on how to assemble a great team, and not only get them but keep them?

Michael: Interestingly, Barbara and I have a disagreement on this particular subject. We've talked about it a few times, the role of self-awareness in an entrepreneur's life. I happen to believe that the more self-aware you are, the more successful you are. Barbara believes the opposite. She believes that good entrepreneurs lack self-awareness because they have to be crazy to continue to go forward. If they're crazy then they're not self-aware. We've debated a little bit about this. She hasn't convinced me and I haven't convinced her, but I happen to believe that that is where self-awareness is probably the most important. Because when you're building a team, a lot of people want to work with their friends or their family, and that's great. However, the key to a good team is understanding your strengths and your weaknesses and building a team around that. I can't tell you how many times I've met co-founders who really have the same skill set and I'm a little unsure when I meet these people why they partner together, because they're both bringing the same thing to the table. So, for me, a good team—and Seth is brilliant on this—is knowing who you work with, but also understanding the depth of experience required, the various facets you need to pull from, and that starts with knowing what you bring to the table and what you do not because we all have a lot of strengths but we also have those weaknesses.

John: We've talked about two of the sharks, Lori and Barbara. Let's just touch base on your impressions of Mark Cuban.

Michael: Mark is the busiest guy I've ever met. That's what I always say. When I need to get interviews with Mark, I have to walk back and forth to the bathroom with him, follow him to the lunch table. He's a really, really passionate investor. He is always engaged. He's always involved and he has a lot of strong opinions, and whether you agree with the opinions or not, I think that's really admirable for somebody whose business is so diversified and he's in so many different areas.

John: Of course, there's Kevin O'Leary, Mr. Wonderful. How did he come up with Mr. Wonderful, do you think?

Michael: Yeah. Actually, when he was doing "Dragons' Den," the Canadian version of "Shark Tank" and someone called him that and it sort of stuck. Kevin is one of my favorite sharks. He's just like you see on TV, a very disciplined, firm businessman. He's a super nice guy. I'm not trying to get after his money, so maybe I have a different perspective on him, but he was the first one to follow me back on social media. He's the first one to email me. I think he's a really good guy and, frankly, I feel more comfortable when I understand an investor's motivation and it's not hidden under pretense and guise. We know who Kevin is, we know what matters to him, and I think there's something admirable, even if it's not popular, being able to say the hard truth and being able to be that person so that people know what they're getting in bed with.

John: If "Shark Tank" has taught us anything, I think it's you can't just have a great idea, you have to know your numbers, right?

Michael: If you're in business, you have to know your numbers. You have to understand where you're heading and where you came from.

John: The issue of valuation, how much your company's worth, especially if it's pre-revenue, and your growth projections, seems to be the biggest thing that trips people up on TV and in real life, actually.

Michael: That's because it's impossible to account for. It really is impossible because there isn't any way to judge a company's success before they've been successful. I mean, there's a lot of ways to make smarter guesses, but it's all guessing.

John: If you've had successful exits, you're a better bet. You're going public or another company buying your company, both in real life and on TV, that really reinforces the shark's confidence in investing with you and maybe even gives you a little bump in your valuation, don't you think?

Michael: Listen, there are many proof points that you can show that whatever you're doing is working in the market is going to help you ultimately. There's no doubt about it. So, if you can come in with some great deals, some great partners, and some great proof, it helps strengthen your valuation and, ultimately, your position in the tank or in front of any investor. But the actual number, that's always hard because it's pretty difficult to know for sure how a business is going to do. I mean, that's part of the risk involved.

John: What I've heard you say about pitching is, deal with your nerves, make sure you're practiced, know your numbers, do your due diligence on the investors, and finally, be likeable. Having a unique personality and make sure it come through. Those are some really great tips here, Michael. I can't thank you enough.

Michael: Well, let me clarify the last tip really quickly. I think this is the most important thing, actually, on how to pitch anything at anytime, anywhere, and it's just this. Are you ready? If someone says, "What's the one thing?" It is this: "Just be a human." I cannot tell you how many times I've watched so many pitches in my life that I see somebody who is charming, smart, magnanimous, great, stand up in front of a group of people and turn into the most boring person in the world. Turn into somebody who, honestly, I wouldn't invest in and I know the person and it is that fear. It is the nerves that kick in, but the fact is, you just have to remember that you're talking to a human, and you are a human. Yeah, what you're talking about is a business. Sure, fine. But, you have to lead by being someone who is relatable, and honest, and authentic, and transparent, and whatever that looks like for you, that's how you lead. You got to go up there and show your personality.

John: I couldn't agree more. One of the things you said earlier was the more self-aware you are, the more successful you are, and I agree with you completely. Is there a book, besides your two wonderful books, that you would recommend people reading to become more self-aware?

Michael: I don't know if I have a book recommendation on self-awareness. What I can tell you is a great book recommendation, as far as learning how to face the fear and how to improve your relationship with doing good work, one of my favorite books of all time is *The War of Art* by Steven Pressfield.

I read it several times a year. It's all about this idea of moving beyond that voice in your head that says, "I can't do this. I'm not fit to do this. There's someone else who could do it better," learning to recognize that voice, to manage that voice, and to move ahead in spite of that voice. So I think that's a book that I really enjoy and, I think, could help people as they move forward. As far as self-awareness, for me, it's practice makes perfect. Every month, we try to get a little better. Every year, we try to get a little better, and really knowing yourself, I happen to think, is the best way to be a good leader and to run a good business.

CLAUDIA IANNAZZO
HOW TO CHARM INVESTORS

Claudia Iannazzo is one of the founding partners at AlphaPrime Ventures, which is a top VC firm. Claudia's background is amazing. It sounds like "The Amazing Race" to me. She's facilitated more than ten billion dollars' worth of acquisitions, divestments, IPOs, and partnerships for public companies around the globe. She started her first company in her undergrad days, and she has a fifteen-year career spanning five continents. She's from England, and she worked in Australia, and now is in New York.

John: I'm excited to get your incredible global perspective on what it takes to be a successful startup and what it takes to get funded. So if you wouldn't mind, would you take us back to those days when you were growing up in England and you decided, "Ah, this is for me – getting into mergers and acquisitions."

Claudia: In the mid-80s, there was a terrible job shortage in the northern hemisphere. My parents moved back to Australia; they're Australian. We landed back in Australia and my father couldn't find a job. He's a civil engineer and a serial entrepreneur. He started a business building and selling patrol boats to the Vietnamese government so that they could patrol up and down their extensive river system. So I'm the daughter of this serial entrepreneur. He's seventy-three now. He emailed me this morning because he wants to do a very big project in Indonesia. I mean, he's a startup junkie. So that was the environment I grew up in. My father knows firsthand the boom, bust, bust, bust, bust, boom. It's a bit rough to be married to an entrepreneur. Then my mother, who is so risk averse; she thinks everybody should go and work for a stable company. So my parents are people from two completely different worlds. I started college when I was seventeen, in Australia. I was holding down three or four jobs paying my own way through college, my tuition, my living. I was waiting tables in a couple of different bars. I was the person in a boutique investment bank where I used to take around the faxes. We used to write the initials of the people who had to read the fax and then take the paper copy around. They read the fax and they hand it back to you, crossed their initials off the paper copy. It was dumb because after kind of four months of doing this job, I just wanted to claw my eyes out with a spoon.

Then when one of the partners in this bank said to me, "Claudia, put the fax down. Take a look at this bid." He was an investment banker helping clients bid a large construction project. When I looked at it, this bid was a Utopian vision of the future. It was this beautiful story as to what we're going to build in this particular property precinct called the Melbourne Dockland's project: beautiful hand-drawn images of this Utopian existence that's going to exist. I took one look at it and I said, "You know what, you're going to have to completely rewrite this." The banker was shocked. "What are you talking about?" I said, "Well, that's going to land on some bureaucrat's desk and the bureaucrat's going to sit there with a bid compliance shopping list and he's going to go, 'Well, where's my community impact study and where's my mercury report and where's my blah-blah-blah,' and he's not going to read three hundred pages to work out where those things are. So if you don't make it easy, you're just going to be excluded."

The investment banker looked at me and said, "Well, Claudia, I don't get paid to rewrite tender submissions." So I said that I'd rewrite it. But he wasn't interested: "I'm not paying you to do that. You're the dumb little kid who delivers my faxes." So I said, "Why don't I pitch your customer?" He said, "You're a teenager." I was. I was an ugly teenager with bad acne. There was nothing pretty about the situation. So he goes, "There's no way I'm letting you pitch my very valued, very big, Asian developer. There's no way." And I said, "Well, how about I get an office, a logo, some business cards, a bunch of old people and I'll get an old person to pitch the customer?" And at this point, I think he just thought the whole situation was ridiculous and he said, "Sure, they'll be here on Thursday." I'm replied, "No problem."

So I borrowed an office from one of my father's friends and I got another friend of my classmate to do a logo and got business cards printed in the middle of the night. I got a bunch of "old" people, older siblings of all my friends. So "old" was thirty. I scripted one of these guys, we pitched the client. The client said, "You know what, I spent a million dollars bidding this particular project. What do you want for a compliance check?" We said, "$15,000?" Something outrageous at the time. And bang, that was my first customer. I had to incorporate the company the next week. Everything happened in the wrong order.

John: Get the customer first, right? I love it.

Claudia: Yeah, get the customer first. Sort out the money. I had to get my dad to be a director in my first company because I was too young, under Australian rules, to even be the CEO of my own company, we took it from there. By the time I finished university, I had a dozen employees servicing customers all around the world. I had huge pressure to open up an office in Asia. I was twenty-one and didn't know what I didn't know. I literally was learning new mistakes every single day. So then I listened to my risk-averse mom who kept saying, "You got to give up this startup thing and get a real job." So I became a mergers acquisitions attorney. I know, terrible idea. Probably the worst thing I've ever done. It's true.

John: Sounds very dry, yes.

Claudia: I met my husband there so it wasn't all bad. After five years of doing that, I said I can't do this anymore. I started a second company in London, a property development company, and that was kind of how my career evolved. Every second role was a startup and the roles in between were with corporates paying the bills. Typically doing deals and negotiations. So I served a wide slew of different roles in different companies, but I've also started a bunch of different companies, which is kind of cool.

John: It's a really great combination of your father's entrepreneurial DNA and your mom's risk aversion to take a job, learn something, go do a startup, go back and forth like that. It's nice. One of the things I already like what you said is if you don't make it easy, you won't get funded. So at a young age, you knew that no one's going to read three hundred pages, and I'm assuming that still holds true to what you look for now as a VC. Well, take us through the differences between working in Australia and America in terms of what the ecosystem is like and how pitches work in those environments.

Claudia: It's so different. My Australian friends tell me it's changed. But I've been in the United States for five years now. When I left Australia, I vowed that I would never start another company in Australia again because we have this culture in Australia of something that we call the tall poppy syndrome. If somebody decides to do something different or have a go at starting a company, we think we're doing them a kindness to point out the three or four reasons why it's absolutely going to fail as an idea. That is very draining for an entrepreneur. Entrepreneurs have to be slightly mad to start companies in the first place. They have to ignore all the conventional wisdom, which says only one in five companies exist four years after founding. So they have to go,

"I'm going to be that one in five," and so to be surrounded by people who are kind of dragging you down the whole time is very demotivating. And it's one of the reasons why I actually think the U.S. has a very vibrant startup ecosystem because people don't talk like that in America. It is completely different experience. They will sit back and go, "What a great idea. Here are two people I can introduce you to." "Have you thought about doing this, this, this, or this to take your idea from being good to great." So it is the exact opposite experience. I am a firm believer of that attitude being the reason why the U.S. can unapologetically say that it is the startup capital of the world at the moment. I think it's the attitude as much as the entrepreneurs and the investors. But it's the attitude of the whole community. In corporates: it's the attitude of a person who will do pilots with startups. And it's the attitude of your next door neighbor who will be encouraging. I think that's a really important difference.

John: It's interesting that you say only one in five businesses are going to make it, so why would you take that risk? The same thing is almost true for marriages, right? And yet we keep doing it. Why would anybody get married if nearly half of marriages are going to fail. You really have to look at this like a business kind of marriage when you decide to invest in these founders.

Claudia: I think it's worse than a marriage actually. I've been married for years. We're happily, deliriously married. However, if my husband irritates me, I can unilaterally divorce him, whereas if I'm an entrepreneur and my investor irritates me, there's very little I can do. I'm stuck with him. Even if I don't want to make them money anymore, I have to make the investor money or else I'm going to be losing all of my own invested money. So it's worse than a marriage. I'm constantly telling entrepreneurs to be super careful about who they take money from. If an investor seems very corrosive or unhelpful in the investment process when they're meant to be courting you and putting their best foot forward, this is as good as it's going to get. They're going to be the most charming when they're trying to convince you to take their check. If in that process, they're ugly, they're going to be hideous as investors.

John: It's going to be much worse.

Claudia: They become members of your family as you build your company.

John: Right, so you have to be discerning, that's for sure. What are the qualities that you look for in a founder because what you do is, if I understand properly, is you look at series B, so someone has already gotten some angel funding of a million or more and has some traction before your company steps in, is that correct?

Claudia: Exactly right. We don't just look to deploy funds; we look to invest in companies where we can do something to improve the revenue. We get actively involved. I roll up the sleeves, I give up my weekends, I give up many days during the week to build the companies that we invest in, which means we don't do a spray and pray. We don't have hundreds of companies in our portfolio. We'll be lucky if we have fifteen to twenty companies in this current portfolio because we get actively involved, which gets to the culture of an entrepreneur and the type of entrepreneur that we'd invest in. Also I won't invest in any entrepreneur who I don't want to buy a beer for. As an Australian, it's easy for me to attribute everything to beer. However, let me explain. Firstly, if I resent spending five bucks on a beer for you, something's gone horribly wrong, and if I don't want to spend the hour with you watching you drink it, it's highly unlikely I'm going to invest in you. So it's really important that entrepreneurs get that it's kind of a charm offensive starting a company: You've got to charm investors to invest in you, even though you really don't have the traction you'd like to have. You've got to charm people to come work for you even though you can't really pay them what they're worth. And you've got to charm customers to put their businesses at risk and engage you in order to use your platform and generate revenues. So if you're not charming when I meet you, I'm going to have big doubts as to whether you can do those three things: investors, staff, and customers.

John: It's all about the likability factor, the charm factor. For me, charm has to do with passion and being interested in what someone else has to say, as opposed to just being interesting. Do you like that definition?

Claudia: I totally agree with you. I like to invest in entrepreneurs who want to have a dialogue with me about it. If they're just going to talk at me and lecture to me, it's probably not worth coming. Our partners come from extremely varied backgrounds. We've all got different connections to bring to the table. We want to introduce our connections to entrepreneurs they will find interesting. That's the kind of model we follow almost every time.

John: What do you think is the number one thing besides cash that the founders need? I mean, your company provides so many things, from refining the value proposition to preparing for an exit. Is there one thing that you go, "Oh, time and time again, this is really what we bring to the table in addition to our funds?"

Claudia: The most important thing to most of our entrepreneurs is our ability to open doors to very important customers for them. So we haven't yet invested in B2C. We're in this B2B space. So what we do is we leverage our own personal connections. These are just really amazing organizations and networks. That's really, I think, probably one of the most influential points with the entrepreneurs. The second thing (and I find I get this feedback quite a lot) is the entrepreneurs want someone who's going to guide them through commercializing their product. Even serial entrepreneurs want help designing and building the right products. I've got one entrepreneur at the moment who's building out a new product road map. They really wanted some help doing this so we ran a workshop on the weekends. More than twenty phenomenal CEOs and product specialists helped them hack their product road map. So these are the kind of things that we can do. Afterwards, this entrepreneur looked at me and said, "This is just phenomenal: I have managed to shortcut my road map development process by a year by just having super smart people help me work through the options." That's the kind of outside the box thinking that we do.

John: Well, that's great. I always love to hear those stories. What also is fascinating to me is before someone can even connect with you, they obviously have had to have some really good connections and some traction to get their seed funding and then they get, probably, a warm introduction to you, I'm guessing, and, from there, what you do is continue to give them more warm introductions to get them customers and help them take their product to the next level, right? So it's continually all about who you know and how you can help people and grow that, right? It's just one network chain after the other.

Claudia: That is true, but only up to a point. I have hundreds of entrepreneurs contact me directly each week. You can use LinkedIn, send me a message or a note. I will answer the phone. My email address is on our website. You click on that email address, and the email comes directly to me. I get entrepreneurs who DM me on Twitter. I do say to all entrepreneurs, "If you can't get to me, you're not trying." When I started my first company, I never raised any money because I didn't know any investors. I didn't know any VCs. The idea of cold calling or cold approaching a VC, well, it fills me with dread. A warm introduction is always the best way if you can get one, but if you can't, don't be afraid if you're contacting the person directly through their website or LinkedIn; they really are on the other end of that email.

John: How many pitches do you think you hear in a year versus the number of ones you actually fund? Is it that 1% number, you think?

Claudia: I see a thousand companies a year. That's my regular deal flow. This year, maybe 1,500. I'll meet with ten companies a week. So that's about five hundred a year. I'll invest in five.

John: There you go. That's what we needed to hear. So, I guess the first issue is, what's your discerning factor from seeing the pitches to deciding, "Okay, I'll meet with these people in person." Is it that they have a really compelling pitch deck that solves the problem that you think is interesting and has potential or is it more about them and the team?

Claudia: Few entrepreneurs, when they meet me, ever get the opportunity to open up their computer to show me their pitch deck because I usually just start saying, "Well, tell me about yourself. What do you do?" and it immediately starts the session. I think you should always have your pitch deck with you because if a particular topic, like competitor landscape, comes up you want to show it and be ready. And then you can email the pitch deck across after. The first thing I'm checking with my opening questions is, are you within our investment mandate? Are you in that seed extension to Series A phase? We're in that early stage. Then, can you tell me what your product is? A lot of entrepreneurs can't even tell me what they do. If you can't tell me, the investor, what you do, you're certainly not going to be able to tell your customer what you do. So I want to hear that they can articulate it. And then, for me, it really then boils down to whether they have really tested the product out, whether that their product is a fit for a large market. We call it product/market fit, which is kind of the shorthand that investors use. But how I look at that is, do you have customers you have signed contracts with, what do those customers say about what you're doing for them, and do those customers see huge value? Because, at the end of the day, for me, if your customers see the value, then your investors will see the value as well. But if your customers don't see the value and if you've got a solution that's looking for a problem to solve, you haven't really worked out the pain point you're solving. You're just going to circle around and not get enough traction. So that's really what I'm looking for.

John: Out of all those people you meet with, do you think you typically have a pretty good gut sense when you're meeting somebody that's like, "Oh, this one has the potential to be one of the five?"

Claudia: I have a real deal flow funnel. I meet five hundred people and a hundred of them I think are interesting and then I'll sleep on it. Fifty of them I'll think are worth looking at closer. So unfortunately, fifty of the people I have a great meeting with are going to get a no at that point. Then, of that remaining fifty, I tend to start to bounce the idea off people, talk to my partners and pass to other investors to see who's interested. We'll move to what we call investigation on about probably fifty companies. We probably get down to maybe ten that I do formal due diligence on. So is there a gut instinct at the start? No. My last two companies that I invested in, my first reaction was I don't quite believe. I couldn't understand what the special sauce was. But I had an investor who was saying to me, "No, Claudia, this is really phenomenal. This is really world-leading," But, in my initial meeting, I didn't get it. It took me a couple of meetings to get it. The second entrepreneur I invested in is interesting. He actually couldn't tell me what his company did. So I had this moment where I was like, "I bet you you're not going to be able to explain what you do to customers." But how wrong was I? In the third meeting, this entrepreneur had neglected to tell me that he was doing more than $10 million in recurring revenues to customers a year. That's just how bad he was at telling a story. He forgot to tell me that he's got $10 million plus worth of happy customers.

John: Well, that's a big take away. Don't bury the lead. If you got some great traction, talk about it. Don't make people dig around or find out later because you usually don't get those second chances. Let me ask you, is there a book that you think founders should read, either about business or life, that could help them through this journey?

Claudia: I'm going to give you an unconventional answer here. I'm not going to say to go read a "how I did it" book. Well, I'm sure there are just phenomenal books out there that will help you network, to grow revenue, I mean, there's a bunch of books out there that are phenomenal for your business, and I did find it valuable to read other founder's books about how they built their business. I think that's interesting. For me, as an entrepreneur, the books I suggest people read are things like Iain Banks. Go read sci-fi and think about technology; the world that we're going to live in, like in fifty years' time, and start thinking about what's needed then. I suspect if you polled VCs, they massively over-index in sci-fi. We're a community of sci-fi geeks. We live in this vision of the future that's in our heads and we're looking for technology that can help solve that future. So, for entrepreneurs, I know it's a bit wacky, but go read some great sci-fi.

John: I love it. I know, because it gets your imagination going and gets you thinking about what's next as opposed to what is. It's great advice. Claudia, thank you for all these insights. The numbers of how you put people through a funnel is really fascinating, as are the kinds of questions that people are going to expect to get asked if they're fortunate enough to get to meet you face to face.

EITAN CHITAYAT
STORYTELLING AND BRANDING

Eitan Chitayat is the founder of natie.com, a boutique branding agency.
He has worked with numerous clients in his career, ranging from AMEX
to Target and Volkswagen, as well as the likes of Facebook, Google,
and Apple, not to mention small startups and medium sized businesses.
He believes that when you are truthful with your brand and your story is
authentic and relevant, the right people will be able to relate to it.
He's got an amazing video that went viral with four million views and
counting called, **"I'm That Jew."** He emphasizes not being
afraid of who you are and putting it out there.

John: Let's start by going back a little. What were you like in college? Did you know that you wanted to get in and be in the creative world? Did you want to do something else or was it always about branding and advertising?

Eitan: I was totally confused when I did my first degree. I actually started in political science, and I minored in English literature. Then I flipped it, majoring in English literature and minoring in political science, and I just really enjoyed that. I moved to Boston to do my master's degree in Integrated Marketing Communications at Emerson College. I've always enjoyed the communications field. It was only in my last semester that I actually, totally by chance, did a creative course in advertising and I kind of got the bug.

As all of my friends were leaving college to get these high-paying jobs in marketing, I sat in the computer lab for six months, and I put pictures with headlines together and shopped a portfolio around. I finally landed a job in advertising and branding as a copywriter on Volkswagen, which was a pretty prestigious account. Being a creative wasn't the plan at the beginning, but it kind of just happened and it was good that it did.

John: It's your own creative process. You've worked with some of the major agencies: OgilvyOne, BBDO, TBWA, which used to be Chiat, and even at Google's Creative Lab. What was it like? What'd you learn at Google?

Eitan: Google was interesting. I mean, I was there as a freelancer. They brought me over to New York City when I was in Israel, and I worked there for a few months. I also worked with the Creative Lab in London and with

Google Africa. The talent at Google is extraordinary and the amazing thing about the New York lab when I was there was that you had direct access to everything that Google is working on that they want to promote.

They found a way under great creative leadership to translate all that crazy technical stuff into things that people can actually feel and understand. It really is crazy technical, some of the things that they're doing there, and to be able to get it across so simply in their communications and in their branding was eye-opening. The creatives that I worked with, some of them were really senior and some of them were really young, so that mix and just being around it was great. I got to work on some incredible things and I'm just very lucky to have been there.

John: People have to somehow figure out a way to take all that tech speak and turn it into a simple pitch for investors. That starts with figuring out your story, a good tagline, logo and overarching brand, which is what you're an expert at. I also want to ask you about what made you decide to go out on your own after working with so many big, prestigious agencies. I'm always fascinated by that kind of decision. What are some of the challenges you've faced that you weren't expecting.

Eitan: I've always been a little bit of a troublemaker, even when I was working at the bigger agencies, and I've always had a pretty strong opinion. When I was working for some of the bigger agencies, I always had a little independent somethin' somethin' going on the side.

When I got back to Israel, I was the Executive Creative Director of TBWA/ Digital for around a year, and within that year, I realized it wasn't working for me. I wasn't able to do the things that I wanted to do, and to be able to deliver the kind of stuff that I was used to delivering, not because there was anything wrong with TBWA/ Digital in Israel. It's more because I came from a different culture and an international background, and TBWA/ Digital was more for the Israeli local market.

So, I decided to just quit and do my own thing. But it wasn't some type of revolution for me because I've always been entrepreneurially inclined. That made it possible for me to work on projects that really allowed me to do what I wanted to do and work with the people that I really wanted to work without having to worry about any other kind of bullshit.

The people I work with who are in my team now are, ultimately, people that I just connect with strategically, creatively, and personally. They kind of get what I want to bring out of whoever I work with in the form of a client. That is super important. When you're creatively driven, to be able to have freedom to work with the people that you want, and get what they give you with their everything—that's huge.

So, the long answer is what I just said. The short answer is I wanted to do what I wanted to do, and that little nugget has always gotten me in trouble, and now it's working for me, which is great. I'm not a Yes man.

John: I want you to speak a little bit more, if you will, because all of the founders, whether they're just starting out and they only have a co-founder and maybe two or three people on their team, eventually want to get funded and grow their company, and you are an expert in finding the right people who fit your culture and your strategy. Can you speak a little bit about how you find the right people that are going to be a corporate fit for where your culture is?

Eitan: I can answer that, minus one word—which is "corporate" because that's the least thing I am. I think you have to find people you instinctively trust. That's the most important thing. I can tell you the best relationships I've had, and the ones I still have, are the ones where you just connect at the gut level. Then, of course, there are the strategic partnerships, the ones where you might not be good at something and the other person fills that gap for you and you do the same thing for them. So, there's that yin and yang thing going there.

Networking is massive. I think one of the things you really need to do if some of your audience is younger is to always stay in touch with everyone you've ever met, because you never know. I mean, there are people I worked with fifteen years ago who I'm still in touch with, and you never know where they're going to end up. If you have a relationship with them and the stars align, then magic might happen. Staying in touch is a very, very important thing.

John: Do you have a process for how you stay in touch with people? Is it through social media or something else?

Eitan: I was in Boston and New York for a while and then, when I went back to Israel, actually, Facebook allowed me to stay on the map, professionally speaking. You know, you write a status and people out there see it and think, "Oh, he's still around. He's still on the radar." So that's definitely helped. I use LinkedIn, too. In general I'm a people person. I'm just a communicative type of guy. So, I just stay in touch with people. It comes naturally to me.

John: It's part of your tagline for natie, so "Communicate. That's what we do." makes complete sense. Since, you've mentioned Facebook, you've actually had Facebook as a client. Can you talk to us about what you learned there or about that culture and branding?

Eitan: I worked with Facebook out of the London Office. We delivered a couple of ideas for Facebook for some of their own clients—to show how social media ideas on their platform could work to great effect. That in itself was interesting because when we did it, which was a couple of years ago, that was new. It was a new way of thinking. We brainstormed for them and with them, and essentially just partnered with them. It wasn't a huge project, and then we did another thing or two. It's great to be able to work with Facebook, Apple, Google, and even YouTube, who we've worked with extensively as well.

John: I also want to ask you about one of the things on your website, which is Valtech. There's an amazing case study in that story, but if you could, tell us about the importance of branding. You have said that strategy is only as good as the first step. The strategy that you had with Valtech, what you were able to do them and matching their design of their product to their complete logo, is completely fascinating and, of course, what an amazing exit.

Eitan: Well, we didn't touch their logo. It's an incredible company. Valtech's doing some amazing things with heart surgery. When they came to us, less than a year ago, they had a logo and a website which was, by their own admission, stuck in the '80s. That's why they came to us. They didn't have much of a written story and they knew that they needed to. They have mind-blowing products, but you couldn't get a sense of that from what you're looking at in their presentation materials, and their old website, and animations that they'd done.

The first thing we did was help them uncover the story they needed to tell. We had extensive, strategic meetings where we realized their truth. And we found out, basically, what makes them tick, how they intend to change the world, and who else is out there not doing the same thing, because no one was doing the same thing. Maybe similar things which led to how they should differentiate themselves.

We were then able to translate that truth into a story that separated them from the rest, that was authentic and relevant to their audience. After that strategy, we developed a consumer-facing or business-to-business and medical industry-facing narrative. Different verticals. Then we evolved the whole brand, visually, from conference materials to brochures to a website. They're doing wonderful things, and it's really nice to work with clients or companies that are changing the world for the better. Valtech's non-invasive heart surgery, to be able to repair someone's heart as it's still beating, is just incredible to work on. I get to work on great stuff. I mean, if you're talking about startups, everyone has an idea and every single idea has potential. So, those are some of the things that we want to work on.

John: Yes: things that can inspire you and your creativity, but then, you're focusing on something creatively, that's helping save lives. What you did for Valtech was make their brand distinctive; you told a story that was authentic and relevant, you said, and that, to me, is what makes people want to invest, whether it's an exit or giving initial funding, and that's what's so fantastic about what you do. This whole concept of storytelling is something I'm constantly working on with my clients when they pitch to get funded. Let's talk about what you do with Entrepreneur Organization in Israel, EO Israel, since that's another whole world of startups. You actually helped them with telling stories. When people hear one or two stories that they can relate to, then they can expand it beyond that, right?

Eitan: With Entrepreneur's Organization Israel, I'm actually a founding chapter member, and I was the Communication Chair for its first two years so I just took it upon myself to do all of the branding, the website, the video, social media and all that stuff. I think it was important to allow our audience, or other potential entrepreneurs in Israel, to understand that we know being an entrepreneur is the loneliest job on the planet. If you're lucky, you do have someone to talk to but, at the end of the day, it's mostly all on you. So, the organization allows you to get some support on a professional level, even on a personal level sometimes. As an entrepreneur, maybe you've been working fourteen hour days for six weeks now and haven't seen your kids. Okay, that's not a professional problem. That becomes a personal problem, a family problem. So, you have people you can talk to about that. Or, you need to hire someone and you've been trying for six months and can't find the right person. You can reach out and get shared experiences that might help you. That's the whole point. So, we did the branding, but it came from within because I'm an entrepreneur and a founding chapter member. It was nice to hit on the truth, knowing the truth, because the people that we are working with are friends and colleagues as well.

John: Yes, the fact that you're a founding member, an entrepreneur yourself, and you can relate to it so well allows you to tell stories that are completely authentic, and again, it's changing the world. The loneliness of the entrepreneur is a problem you're solving with EO, correct?

Eitan: It's a global organization of around eleven thousand members and what they have done is put entrepreneurs together to support each other. It's not really a support group. You support each other just because you're like-minded people, you know? I think that's really important when you work this way. I mean, my agency is a core team of four or five people and a couple of stellar remote teams who are literally part of the team. That's our structure. So, if I want to make a big decision for my business, I can reach out to a few people within the Israel chapter alone, who also have small teams but work with very big businesses. I mean, you can reach out to people in different countries who are part of the organization. When you fly to London, if you want, you can reach out to chapter members there and just say, "Hey, I'm an EO global member, what's going on in London?" and nine times out of ten, people reach back out to you and say, "Hey, come and meet me." It's also a networking organization, too. They have big events that people from all around the world go to, universities, programs, seminars.

John: It reminds me of American Express with global offices, and you can always have a place, almost like a second embassy, if you're traveling, and need a soft place to land, so to speak. That's a soft place to land for entrepreneurs who might be visiting other countries.

Eitan: I've heard really nice stories about people who have been there for complete strangers just because of this organization, this connection, this platform, whatever you want to call it. I mean, at the end of the day, it's all about people. If we're talking about entrepreneurs and startups, and you've brought up storytelling, I think one of the most important things, really, is to get your story right. When it comes to branding, getting your story right has nothing to do, really, with creativity at its core. It's about understanding who you are and what you're doing, and then translating that into a narrative of words, visuals and spreading it via different mediums like animations and websites and stuff. But, the brand story is uncovering the truth of who you are. Branding is about getting to the bottom of who you are and I like that.

John: I do, too. Well, you've gone from using storytelling to help Valtech save lives with heart surgery to helping EO Israel help entrepreneurs with a place for shared resources to this amazing viral video that you've created to also help, not only yourself, but you're telling a story in your viral video,

"I'm That Jew." How many people have watched this? Everyone's always looking for something they can make go viral, but I don't think that was your intent when you started.

Eitan: Well, first of all, I'm happy that you're asking about it and that's great. I mean, I'm happy to talk about it. Within six weeks, "I'm That Jew" had around four million views. But it's not the number. It's the comments that have been the most moving. So, there's like tens of thousands of comments and they're amazing and moving. It started off as a blog post that I put out there, as a written narrative. After the Charlie Hebdo massacre in Paris, some terrorists killed some Jewish shoppers at a kosher supermarket and I wrote a narrative about it. In time, I just realized I wanted to present it as a visual story.

So, it was written by me, a Jew, to my Jewish brothers and sisters, but also to anyone who shouldn't be afraid, whether you're black, or gay, a woman, transgender; whoever you are, own it and be proud of it. It's meant to be a celebration of who we are. You should just be able to say what you are and hope that the people out there who are listening will embrace it. We can embrace our differences. In this case, though, I was saying it directly to the Jewish people from me. Actually, I was saying it to a woman who is living in France right after the time of those massacres and who was just afraid to say that she was Jewish. She's a friend of mine. I basically wrote it based on a conversation we had and then I produced it with some just really close-knit group of friends, family and colleagues and put it out there one night. I knew that people would spread it. I just didn't think that it would have this kind of impact. The response has been so emotional. I've cried several times because of some of the things that people have written.

John: I think it's totally relevant to what we're talking about, which is storytelling is understanding the truth of who you are and you were brave enough to put that story out there. It reminds me of Elizabeth Gilbert's *Eat, Pray, Love.* She talks about how she wrote that book for one specific friend of hers who couldn't travel because she had a husband and children. So, she filtered everything. And you created "I'm that Jew" for your one friend who was afraid to say she was Jewish. So, there was a real specific audience and intention. The other thing that you touched on is really encouraging people not to be afraid. I read that that's one of your key criteria of who you like to hire, creatively, is that they're not afraid to take chances and risks. So, I think it's full circle, right?

Eitan: Yeah, that's funny. I mean, not being afraid gets me into trouble a lot of the time. I'm not talking about putting stuff like "I'm That Jew" out there. I'm talking about sometimes butting heads with clients and partners and colleagues. But I think you have to be who you are. You have to not be afraid to have faith in who you are and to trust your instincts and to put yourself out there. The right person who is opposite you, if it is the right person, will somehow be able to embrace that or take what you're saying or be able to take you in another direction. The fact that you are authentic, not afraid, can work on your behalf.

It can get you in trouble, but it's a quality that I look for. The designer on our team from Italy challenges me all the time, but in the most respectful way. It's not easy to challenge. My strategist, today, called me up and, after meeting with the client, we were disagreeing, openly, in front of the client, but it was all in the pursuit of what we think the client needs the most. It's not always easy to be honest in this world. To not conform. Do you know what I mean?

John: Yes, I do. That leads me into my last question for you. Tell me about The 5 Percent Club.

Eitan: The 5 Percent Club is a platform, a social media platform, and it allows people to express what they're really feeling. The idea is, if 95% of your life is on autopilot, like you going to work, taking the kids to school, eating with friends, the ordinary stuff, then the remaining 5% isn't. It's the stuff that really means a lot to you. It's that something you really feel in the depth of your soul, or the thing you're dying to say, the experience you went through that is changing your life. Something maybe you haven't really talked about before. That's the 5%. And that's what we ask you to talk about on the site. Someone recently wrote an article about not finding the time to reminisce each beautiful year that goes by with her family. So she takes the time, once a year, to go through her photo albums and put together an album. And, in doing that, she connects with the year that she just had. Someone else wrote about a custody battle that he had with his ex-wife, where the judge told him basically, "You know, because you're a man, you won't get custody. Kids should be with their mother." So he wrote about that. (And he won the custody battle.)

Things that really affect you and move you: that's the idea of The 5 Percent Club. It allows you to share and to play your meaningful experience forward. It's a small initiative. It's a project I hope will gain traction in time.

JULIA PIMSLEUR
MILLION DOLLAR WOMEN

Julia Pimsleur is the founder of Little Pim, an education tech company that produces the leading foreign language teaching program for kids. She raised over five million dollars between angels and venture capitalists to get her company into the multi-millions in revenues. She is also the author of *Million Dollar Women,* with a goal of helping one million women break one million in revenue by 2020. Julia is just the person to do it.

Julia: I'm happy to talk about raising money. That's one of my favorite topics! I'm one of these weird people who like to raise money.

John: We will dig into that, but before we do, I want to always find out about your passion. How did you become so passionate about this? Tell me more about what Little Pim does, and how that relates to your father, because it's such an interesting journey. How does someone become so successful and raise money? What is the motivation behind it? How did you get this passion? Did it come from your father?

Julia: I never thought I would be a business person, actually. I was a creative person. In college, I studied film and women's studies. I was a documentary filmmaker for many years. I grew up bilingual in French and English, and that's something that just opened so many doors for me throughout my life. I felt like it was the best gift that my parents ever gave me. When my own son was born about eleven years ago, I went out looking for a great language teaching program to help him learn a second language at the age kids learn best, which is up to age six. I couldn't believe there was nothing on the market for very little kids. All the studies show, that's the best time for them to learn a language. Drawing on my filmmaking background, and also being the daughter of Dr. Paul Pimsleur, who invented a language teaching method for adults, I decided to create the first-ever language teaching method for very young children, Little Pim.

John: You know what I love about that already is it's a personal problem you're solving that has multiple implications. You know for yourself that being bilingual changed your life.

Julia: It's true that being bilingual is an incredible benefit and I reaped rewards from that in so many areas from scholarships to being able to live and work abroad. For me, helping parents be their kids' first language tutor is also about democratizing foreign language learning. If you look out over the landscape, the one percent have always figured out a way to have their kids learn Spanish, or Mandarin, or French. In the public school system, kids start as late as fifth grade or middle school, learning a language. Then, most of us really never learn, right? That's what I hear from a lot of parents. They never really mastered a second language. It's because they're starting too late.

John: Well, Little Pim fills that important niche, which shows why it's such a great enterprise. Let me ask you about something you say in *Million Dollar Women* that I really resonated with. You talk about the need for grit, and how to get off the entrepreneur hamster wheel.

Julia: Sure. I was just working so hard and running, running, running in my business in the first few years, which I think is typical when you're getting your business off the ground. I didn't stop to look up and think about what the business could be if I had twice as much funding, if I had different partners, if I really embraced the idea of going big. Once I finally did that, I call that getting off the entrepreneur's hamster wheel. It's like, stop running so fast and take a minute to think about where you're trying to go. Then I realized I really needed capital in order to go to the next level. That's what started the journey of raising venture capital, which ultimately lead me to write *Million Dollar Women*. I love in Michael Gerber's *The E-Myth* when he says, "You need to work on the business, not in the business." For so many of us, that means taking a step back and figuring out what does this company look like at scale? How am I going to get there?

John: Tell us of that great story of how prepared you were. That's what I love, because I'm constantly working with my clients on preparation, getting them to understand that they have to be confident and ready when an opportunity arises. Would you take us back to that story?

Julia: I spent about nine months getting ready to raise venture capital, watching videos on YouTube, episodes of "Shark Tank," talking to any CEO who had raised venture capital who would share their experiences with me. All that time was time away from my business, time away from my two little boys, and my family. I just felt, "Gosh, this should be easier. Why is it so hard to figure out how to raise capital?" When I finally raised my 2.1 million dollars, and it was really the hardest thing I ever did, I have to say, maybe next to childbirth. So, I knew then that I wanted to work to make this easier for other women. I started by creating a little fundraising boot camp in my conference room in New York, where I would help ten women at a time learn how to raise angel and venture capital. Their stories are what inspired me to write *Million Dollar Women* to try to help thousands, and eventually millions of women, learn how to raise capital and take their businesses big.

John: Fundraising boot camp: I like that because you really do have to be prepared as if you're going to battle. One of the terms in the military, which I think is always so interesting is, you don't rise to the occasion, you fall back on your training, right? You can't just think, "Oh, I'll just wing it when I pitch." You have to be trained, correct?

Julia: That's so true, and you also have to be really ready to just find a way no matter what. I remember I was out pitching and I would spend half my day, every day, going to the offices of these VCs and showing my PowerPoint and telling my story over and over again. One day, I came back from a particularly demoralizing meeting where we got a big 'no' right away. I walked into my office, and I saw my head of sales and my head of marketing hunkered down, planning our holiday marketing campaign. I just thought, "you know what? I have to raise this money. They can't do it, I have to do it." That day it became a 'when' and not an 'if.' I think that might have made all the difference, that I really fully committed and said "I don't care if I have to meet another fifty people, I'm going to find this money and they deserve it, and we deserve it. I'm just going it make it happen." Even though it may take months, I knew I'd get it done. I had to. Fundraising is brutal, it really is. As women, we face additional challenges because we often don't have the kind of networks that some of our male counterparts do where we can just pick up the phone and have an easy entree to someone in a VC firm. Also, frankly, women face discrimination here and there, sometimes unconscious and sometimes the old school, overt kind. I wanted to help women, to make it much easier for them to go raise money, much easier than it was for me. I do think that because women are newer to the fundraising game that we have a lot of catching up to do. The book I wrote is to help women catch up more quickly. I think the biggest obstacle for women in raising money is simply not knowing the fundraising dance. Having been a professional fundraiser in the non-profit world for several years before I went out raising money for Little Pim, I can say that that even for me, it was totally intimidating. It is a whole new set of vocabulary to learn, and I want to help women master that much more quickly so that we can get the 4% number up at least into the double digits (only 4% of venture capital gets invested in women-run businesses).

John: Well, I love the fact that you call it a fundraising dance. Just calling it a dance somehow takes the edge off of it, just a little bit. If we think of it as a dance, and the conversation, and the negotiation, and all that due diligence, and all that good stuff is a dance, and much like preparing for a dance, you're probably want to rehearse the steps before you go out on the dance floor, right?

Julia: Absolutely, and the truth is that one of the ways that raising money is like a dance is that you have to do the dance that is already happening on the dance floor. You can't go to a salsa dance and start doing the tango, right? I think the best thing for women to realize is that venture capital has been functioning a certain way for many, many years. While we think that landscape could change as more women become VCs and become investors, for now, we have to dance the dance that's already being danced. It's not as hard as you think, but it does need to be explained and practiced. Then, women can be just as successful as men on the dance floor.

John: One of the things in *Million Dollar Women* that I really loved was how prepared you were when the opportunity presented itself for you to whip out financials to show somebody who had indicated some interest. Then, you heard those magic eight words. Would you tell us about that?

Julia: Yes. The magic eight words were, "I can help you find a million dollars." Any entrepreneur would love to hear that. That was back in my angel capital fundraising days. I sat down with a friend of the family who had actually given me my first job in high school. He was pretty much the only person I knew in the banking world, which speaks again to women and their networks. Even though I went to an Ivy League college, and I have a lot of friends who are consultants, and lawyers, I didn't actually know anyone in banking, or in the investment world. So I sat down with this friend of the family who had known I was growing Little Pim and had watched me working two jobs, and getting out our first videos, and setting everything up. I said to him, "I think I'm ready to go full time, you know? We made close to $80,000 in our first year without anyone even working full time in the company. And, there's such a high demand for language learning. Do you have any resources for me?" I thought he'd tell me about a government grant, or something I could apply for. Instead he said, "I can help you find a million dollars." Thus my angel investing dance began. He and I went out and pitched. Well, I pitched, but he made a lot of the introductions to raise the first million for me to fund Little Pim.

John: That's such a great story. The big takeaways are 1) you talked about the traction you already have, and 2) how big the market was, all in one sentence. That's really so succinct and compelling, that those are the key things people are looking for in addition to, of course, investing in you.

If someone has known you since high school, they know you're a go-getter, and tenacity is your key strength.

Julia: That really helped, and I also think that hearing that we had already sold so many without even putting any marketing dollars in was critical. I always think of cash as like the gas that you put in the tank of your car. You can't go very far very fast if you don't have much gas in the tank. So, for him to hear that we'd already made this traction without really having anything in the tank gave him the idea that if we filled it up, we could go pretty far, pretty fast, which we did. We grew so much once we raised that capital, and then after the venture capital, doubled our sales again. That was exciting.

John: Hitting those milestones. What advice do you have directly about pitching, since you run a funding boot camp? Are there certain key elements that you work with, the women who are in your funding boot camp, on their pitch that you could share with us?

Julia: One of the key things about pitching is knowing how to credential yourself. This is an area where women sometimes don't come off as powerfully as men, where I've had women who get up and pitch. They say, "I have this great idea, and I'm going to start this new bio-tech company." Twenty minutes later they mention at the end that they have a PhD! It's like, if you have a PhD and you're running a science company, you should probably mention that right up front. So, for women to really own their domain expertise and be able to talk about why they are the right person to start this company and to take it to scale, is really important.

Sometimes women are nervous that if they haven't already grown a multi-million dollar company, that they'll have trouble getting the credibility they need. The truth is that investors are listening for much more than just what's the last company you took public, right? If you've done that, great, but very few people have. They want to know when have you been in a situation in your professional life where you had to just give it everything and get through really tough challenges.

That's what being an entrepreneur is, and the investors know it. They want to hear that you have that total commitment. You've got the grit, even if it's something in your personal life. I met with a young woman the other day who's starting a company to help people take care of loved ones who have illnesses, terminal illnesses. She grew up with a mom with MS. Since she was nine years old, she's been taking care of her mom who had MS. Now she's creating a website and a platform to help other people taking care of people with terminal illnesses. That's powerful. I can't imagine what she went through taking care of her mother as a child. This woman has grit.

John: Yes, that's such a great story. It really gives the element of what makes someone memorable. I bet that's really one of the key things that I find consistently is if you put yourself in the shoes of an investor, you have a little empathy for them. They hear multiple pitches a day. What is it about you and your story that's going to make you memorable? You clearly check off all those boxes, I'm sure, that's why you got your funding, but is there anything else that you can add to that?

Julia: I think telling stories that the investors can remember is really critical. Whether it's about a customer who loved your service, or it's about some kind of amazing traction that you got because you remember the investors are going to have to show this information with their team, and probably their probably inner circle whether it's the LPs that they're reporting to, their limited partnerships. Or, even their wives and families, right? Why are you interested in this company? I always tell people to think about what would the investor say at the cocktail party that he's going to the night after he's heard your pitch? If he can't think of one story, or if she can't think of one example that you gave that's memorable, then you should think about adding that in because you might get forgotten among the hundred other pitches and stories that he or she heard that day.

John: That's so great. I love that concept of imagining the investor at a cocktail party and saying, "I heard a ton of pitches this week, but one of them really stuck with me. Let me tell you this story about XYZ," right? In fact, one of the other investors that I interviewed said, "You should grab my heartstrings and pull hard," and you've just shared a great example of that, Julia. Thank you.

Julia: You know, a way to practice that actually is if you can find a friend who's an investor, but not an investor in your area. For example, I pitched to someone in bio-tech because Little Pim has nothing to do with bio-tech. After you pitch—even if it is just on the phone—then ask, "Give me ten minutes, please. Tell me what you just heard." Have them pitch your company back to you, and see what actually got through, and that's a great way to know if you're telling your story in a memorable way. It could be brutal, but you'll learn important stuff about your pitch.

John: Well, it's the truth, and better to come from someone like that than the real thing. So, practice your pitch by practicing it to somebody not investing in your niche and let them tell you back what they heard, or where they got confused because the confused mind always says "no." The minute you confuse somebody, you've lost them. It's really great feedback. A great tip. Julia, in addition to your own wonderful book, *Million Dollar Women,* are there any other books that you would recommend?

Julia: I love Brad Feld's *Venture Deals.* That's like the Bible for me, and Mark Peter Davis came out with an awesome book called *Fundraising Rules.* He's a VC who, after hearing so many pitches and realizing that people just didn't even know the fundamentals of pitching to VCs, gave us a gift and put in his book actual phrases that would help when you're meeting with a VC, how to respond to specific questions. I find that's really helpful. I often thought about learning the venture capital dance as trying to become conversational in another language, maybe because I run a language teaching company, that was a metaphor that worked for me. It was helpful to think, "I don't have to be fluent in this language, right? I'm already running a business. I have expertise in other areas," but I have to be conversational. That is so important for people going out to pitch, and it's part of the dance, frankly. You have to learn their steps, and part of that is knowing how to answer questions about liquidation preferences, discounts, and rates of return, and everything that they're dealing with every single day.

John: It's such a great analogy, especially from you because you're an expert in languages, that you don't have to be completely fluent, but you have to be conversational in the language that the VCs and angels talk in. That's great.

Julia: I think it lowers the stakes a little bit. I know that for a lot of people, fundraising is just really terrifying and they would rather have a root canal. The other thing to remember is that the investors don't expect you to be experts in their world. They expect you to be expert in your world. I always tell people, "Own your domain expertise. You don't have to pretend that you're good at everything. If you do, then they're going to doubt your integrity. No one's good at everything." I suggest you should own the things you are good at, and then be very transparent about how you're getting help with the rest, whether it's coaches, mentors, or surrounding yourself with an amazing team. I just really want to help make it easier for other women (and men) who are fundraising, and I want to see a million women get to a million in revenues by 2020. Let's make that happen together!

ACKNOWLEDGMENTS

My gratitude to my family who always supports me in my dreams to make a difference with my life and career. My husband Oscar, my sister Barbara and my Mom are the people who have my back no matter what.

My business partners in *Crack The Funding Code* Judy Robinett and Dee Burgess who inspire me daily to help startups get funded. I am so grateful we are in each other lives.

My thanks also go to my book publisher, publicist and friend Steve Rohr as well as my amazing editor Chris Freeman. Your insights and expertise are priceless. Special thanks to Sergio Belletini for the amazing cover design and layout as well to Harry Duran at Fullcast.co who edits and produces *The Successful Pitch* podcast. Thanks to Helen Irwin for her proofreading skills.

A special thanks to all the guests of my podcasts, but especially the ten that are featured here in this book.

To all my friends who help cheer me on and give me so much joy, a heartfelt thanks with a special shout out to Tracy Leigh Hazzard, Richard Ayoub, Nick Urbom, Jim Chabin, Kevin Bailey, James Mellon, Will and Nora Rose-Hines, Phillip Sherman, Tina and Dave Payne, Michael Corbett, Scott Anderson and Jose De Jesus Pena, Joe Argazzi, Eric Handler, Tim Robinson and Bob Cohen, John Gile, Jerry, Hunter and Kym Douglas, Lawrence Zarian, Gary Bergevin, Mark Margolis, Jeffrey Young, Brooks Oldridge, Jessica Rhodes, Monica DeAlba, Dr. Sudip Bose, Luke Yankee, Don Hill, Angella Nazarian, Lynn Rosenthal, Dana Levan, John Allen, Amy Armstrong, Claudia DeJesus, Ken Best, Kasey Bryant, Ken Baker, Cole Smith, Tim Corrigan, Nicholas Creswell, Nicholas Ayre, Elaine Gordon, Erin Haskell, Jay and Marcella Kerwin, Elissa Goodman, Rolonda Watts, Jason and Heather Powers, Judith Light, Rick Tamlyn and Chuck Loi, Paul Livesay, Sheila Burns, John and Susie Scavo, Brooke and Zaven Ghanimian, Chris Van Meter, Rada Maksimovic, Narb and Nancy Avedissian, Diane Silberstein, Nina Lawrence, Alyce Alston, Fatima Lowes-Williams, and Navid Dayzad.

ABOUT THE AUTHOR

As a funding strategist, **John Livesay** helps CEOs craft a compelling pitch that engages investors in a way that inspires them to join a startup's team. He is partners with **Judy Robinett** in *Crack the Funding Code* which gets founders funded fast. He hosts *"The Successful Pitch"* podcast with investors from around the world. He is the *Pitch Mentor* at **Startfast.net,** the number one accelerator in Upstate New York.

After a successful twenty year career in media sales with *Conde Nast* where he worked across all twenty-two brands in their corporate division, John was named Salesperson of the Year in 2012. The way he was able to win that award was through creating a collaborative partnership with **Guess** jeans that resulted in a joint anniversary celebration for both **Guess** 30th and *W* magazine's 40th. Images of celebrities such as **Drew Barrymore,** who appeared on the cover *W* and was a **Guess** model, were shown at an event celebrating both brands' anniversary. The press generated from this event, along with the exclusive insert of thirty pages of **Guess** models bundled with *W's* anniversary issue, made for an unprecedented partnership that was a win-win for both brands.

John has appeared in *INC.* magazine and on **CBS News** and *"Talk of the Town"* as a confidence expert and the media has called him *"The Pitch Whisperer."*

CPSIA information can be obtained
at www.ICGtesting.com
Printed in the USA
LVOW01s0817020517
532927LV00031B/1885/P